CONFEDERATE MONUMENTS

It is the duty we owe to the dead, the
dead who died for us, but whose
memories can never die. It is a duty
we owe to posterity to see that our
children shall know the virtues and
rise worthy of their sires.

JEFFERSON DAVIS

᭣ THE LOCHLAINN SEABROOK COLLECTION ᭢

AMERICAN CIVIL WAR
Abraham Lincoln Was a Liberal, Jefferson Davis Was a Conservative: The Missing Key to Understanding the American Civil War
Confederacy 101: Amazing Facts You Never Knew About America's Oldest Political Tradition
Confederate Blood and Treasure: An Interview With Lochlainn Seabrook
Everything You Were Taught About African-Americans and the Civil War is Wrong, Ask a Southerner!
Everything You Were Taught About the Civil War is Wrong, Ask a Southerner!
Give This Book to a Yankee! A Southern Guide to the Civil War For Northerners
Lincoln's War: The Real Cause, the Real Winner, the Real Loser
The Great Yankee Coverup: What the North Doesn't Want You to Know About Lincoln's War!
The Ultimate Civil War Quiz Book: How Much Do You Really Know About America's Most Misunderstood Conflict?
Women in Gray: A Tribute to the Ladies Who Supported the Southern Confederacy

CONFEDERATE MONUMENTS
Confederate Monuments: Why Every American Should Honor Confederate Soldiers and Their Memorials

CONFEDERATE FLAG
Confederate Flag Facts: What Every American Should Know About Dixie's Southern Cross

SECESSION
All We Ask Is To Be Let Alone: The Southern Secession Fact Book

SLAVERY
Everything You Were Taught About American Slavery is Wrong, Ask a Southerner!
Slavery 101: Amazing Facts You Never Knew About America's "Peculiar Institution"

CHILDREN
Honest Jeff and Dishonest Abe: A Southern Children's Guide to the Civil War
Saddle, Sword, and Gun: A Biography of Nathan Bedford Forrest For Teens

NATHAN BEDFORD FORREST
A Rebel Born: A Defense of Nathan Bedford Forrest - Confederate General, American Legend (winner of the 2011 Jefferson Davis Historical Gold Medal)
A Rebel Born: The Screenplay
Forrest! 99 Reasons to Love Nathan Bedford Forrest
Give 'Em Hell Boys! The Complete Military Correspondence of Nathan Bedford Forrest
Nathan Bedford Forrest and African-Americans: Yankee Myth, Confederate Fact
Nathan Bedford Forrest and the Battle of Fort Pillow: Yankee Myth, Confederate Fact
Nathan Bedford Forrest and the Ku Klux Klan: Yankee Myth, Confederate Fact
Nathan Bedford Forrest: Southern Hero, American Patriot - Honoring a Confederate Icon and the Old South
Saddle, Sword, and Gun: A Biography of Nathan Bedford Forrest For Teens
The Quotable Nathan Bedford Forrest: Selections From the Writings and Speeches of the Confederacy's Most Brilliant Cavalryman

QUOTABLE SERIES
The Alexander H. Stephens Reader: Excerpts From the Works of a Confederate Founding Father
The Quotable Alexander H. Stephens: Selections From the Writings and Speeches of the Confederacy's First Vice President
The Quotable Jefferson Davis: Selections From the Writings and Speeches of the Confederacy's First President
The Quotable Nathan Bedford Forrest: Selections From the Writings and Speeches of the Confederacy's Most Brilliant Cavalryman
The Quotable Robert E. Lee: Selections From the Writings and Speeches of the South's Most Beloved Civil War General
The Quotable Stonewall Jackson: Selections From the Writings and Speeches of the South's Most Famous General
The Unquotable Abraham Lincoln: The President's Quotes They Don't Want You To Know!

CONSTITUTIONAL HISTORY
The Articles of Confederation Explained: A Clause-by-Clause Study of America's First Constitution
The Constitution of the Confederate States of America Explained: A Clause-by-Clause Study of the
    South's Magna Carta

VICTORIAN CONFEDERATE LITERATURE
Rise Up and Call Them Blessed: Victorian Tributes to the Confederate Soldier, 1861-1901
The Old Rebel: Robert E. Lee As He Was Seen By His Contemporaries
Victorian Confederate Poetry: The Southern Cause in Verse, 1861-1901

ABRAHAM LINCOLN
Abraham Lincoln: The Southern View - Demythologizing America's Sixteenth President
Lincolnology: The Real Abraham Lincoln Revealed in His Own Words - A Study of Lincoln's
    Suppressed, Misinterpreted, and Forgotten Writings and Speeches
The Great Impersonator! 99 Reasons to Dislike Abraham Lincoln
The Unholy Crusade: Lincoln's Legacy of Destruction in the American South
The Unquotable Abraham Lincoln: The President's Quotes They Don't Want You To Know!

CIVIL WAR BATTLES
Encyclopedia of the Battle of Franklin - A Comprehensive Guide to the Conflict that Changed the
    Civil War
Nathan Bedford Forrest and the Battle of Fort Pillow: Yankee Myth, Confederate Fact

PARANORMAL
Carnton Plantation Ghost Stories: True Tales of the Unexplained from Tennessee's Most Haunted
    Civil War House!
UFOs and Aliens: The Complete Guidebook

FAMILY HISTORIES
The Blakeneys: An Etymological, Ethnological, and Genealogical Study - Uncovering the Mysterious
    Origins of the Blakeney Family and Name
The Caudills: An Etymological, Ethnological, and Genealogical Study - Exploring the Name and
    National Origins of a European-American Family
The McGavocks of Carnton Plantation: A Southern History - Celebrating One of Dixie's Most Noble
    Confederate Families and Their Tennessee Home

MIND, BODY, SPIRIT
Autobiography of a Non-Yogi: A Scientist's Journey From Hinduism to Christianity (Dr. Amitava
    Dasgupta, with Lochlainn Seabrook)
Britannia Rules: Goddess-Worship in Ancient Anglo-Celtic Society - An Academic Look at the
    United Kingdom's Matricentric Spiritual Past
Christ Is All and In All: Rediscovering Your Divine Nature and the Kingdom Within
Christmas Before Christianity: How the Birthday of the "Sun" Became the Birthday of the "Son"
Jesus and the Gospel of Q: Christ's Pre-Christian Teachings As Recorded in the New Testament
Jesus and the Law of Attraction: The Bible-Based Guide to Creating Perfect Health, Wealth, and
    Happiness Following Christ's Simple Formula
Seabrook's Bible Dictionary of Traditional and Mystical Christian Doctrines
The Bible and the Law of Attraction: 99 Teachings of Jesus, the Apostles, and the Prophets
The Book of Kelle: An Introduction to Goddess-Worship and the Great Celtic Mother-Goddess
    Kelle, Original Blessed Lady of Ireland
The Goddess Dictionary of Words and Phrases: Introducing a New Core Vocabulary for the
    Women's Spirituality Movement
The Way of Holiness: The Story of Religion and Myth From the Cave Bear Cult to Christianity

WOMEN
Aphrodite's Trade: The Hidden History of Prostitution Unveiled
Princess Diana: Modern Day Moon-Goddess - A Psychoanalytical and Mythological Look at Diana
    Spencer's Life, Marriage, and Death (with Dr. Jane Goldberg)
Women in Gray: A Tribute to the Ladies Who Supported the Southern Confederacy

Five-Star Books & Gifts From the Heart of the American South
SeaRavenPress.com

CONFEDERATE MONUMENTS

Why Every American Should Honor Confederate Soldiers and Their Memorials

☆ A PICTORIAL PRIMER ☆

GENEROUSLY ILLUSTRATED BY THE AUTHOR,
"THE VOICE OF THE TRADITIONAL SOUTH," COLONEL

LOCHLAINN SEABROOK

JEFFERSON DAVIS HISTORICAL GOLD MEDAL WINNER

Diligently Researched for the Elucidation of the Reader

2018

Sea Raven Press, Nashville, Tennessee, USA

CONFEDERATE MONUMENTS

Published by
Sea Raven Press, Cassidy Ravensdale, President
PO Box 1484, Spring Hill, Tennessee 37174-1484 USA
SeaRavenPress.com • searavenpress@gmail.com

SEA RAVEN PRESS
SOUTHERN BOOKS, REAL HISTORY!

1st SRP paperback edition, 1st printing: March 2018, ISBN: 978-1-943737-62-8
1st SRP hardcover edition, 1st printing: March 2018, ISBN: 978-1-943737-63-5

ISBN: 978-1-943737-63-5 (hardcover)
Library of Congress Control Number: 2018934102

Confederate Monuments: Why Every American Should Honor Confederate Soldiers and Their Memorials, by Lochlainn Seabrook. Includes an index, endnotes, and bibliographical references.

Front and back cover design and art, book design, layout, and interior art by Lochlainn Seabrook.
All images, graphic design, graphic art, and illustrations copyright © Lochlainn Seabrook.
All images selected, placed, manipulated, and/or created by Lochlainn Seabrook.
Cover photo: Robert E. Lee, equestrian statue; design © Lochlainn Seabrook.

The views on the American "Civil War" documented in this book are those of the publisher.

PRINTED & MANUFACTURED IN OCCUPIED TENNESSEE, FORMER CONFEDERATE STATES OF AMERICA

SEA RAVEN PRESS

Dedication

To our gallant Confederate dead, whom God's finger has touched:

Ever honored,
Ever loved,
Ever cherished.

They fought defending American freedom; unsurpassed in the annals
of war for heroism, endurance of hardship, and patriotic devotion.

Epigraph

The time has now come, in the evolution of sentiment and feeling, under the providence of God, when, in the spirit of fraternity, we should share with you in the care of the graves of the Confederate soldiers.

U.S. PRESIDENT AND FORMER UNION SOLDIER,

William McKinley

ATLANTA, GEORGIA, DECEMBER 14, 1898

CONTENTS

THERE'S GLORY IN GLOOM

Yes, give me the land where the ruins are spread,
And the living tread on the hearts of the dead;
Yes, give me a land that is blessed by the dust,
And bright with the deeds of the down-trodden just;
Yes, give me the land where the battle's red blast
Has flashed on the future the form of the past;
Yes, give me a land that hath legends and lays
That tell of the memories of long-vanished days;
Yes, give me a land that hath story and song
To tell of the strife of the right with the wrong;
Yes, give me the land with a grave in each spot,
And names in the graves that shall not be forgot;
Yes, give me the land of the wreck and the tomb—
There's grandeur in graves, there's glory in gloom;
For out of the gloom future brightness is born,
As after the night looms the sunrise of morn;
And the graves of the dead, with the grass overgrown,
May yet form the footstool of liberty's throne.
And each single wreck in the warpath of might
Shall yet be a rock in the temple of right.[1]

FATHER ABRAM JOSEPH RYAN
NASHVILLE, TENNESSEE, 1878

NOTES TO THE READER

"NOTHING IN THE PAST IS DEAD TO THE MAN WHO WOULD
LEARN HOW THE PRESENT CAME TO BE WHAT IT IS."

WILLIAM STUBBS, VICTORIAN ENGLISH HISTORIAN

THE TWO MAIN POLITICAL PARTIES IN 1860

☞ In any study of America's antebellum, bellum, and postbellum periods, it is vitally important to understand that in 1860 the two major political parties—the Democrats and the newly formed Republicans—were the opposite of what they are today. In other words, the Democrats of the mid 19th Century were Conservatives, akin to the Republican Party of today, while the Republicans of the mid 19th Century were Liberals, akin to the Democratic Party of today.[2]

Thus the Confederacy's Democratic president, Jefferson Davis, was a Conservative (with libertarian leanings); the Union's Republican president, Abraham Lincoln, was a Liberal (with socialistic leanings).[3]

The author's cousin, Confederate Vice President and Democrat Alexander H. Stephens: a Southern Conservative.

This is why, in the mid 1800s, the conservative wing of the Democratic Party was known as "the States' Rights Party."[4]

Hence, the Democrats of the Civil War period referred to themselves as "conservatives," "confederates," "anti-centralists," or "constitutionalists" (the latter because they favored strict adherence to the original Constitution—which tacitly guaranteed states' rights—as created by the Founding Fathers), while the Republicans called themselves "liberals," "nationalists," "centralists," or "consolidationists" (the latter three because they wanted to nationalize the central government and consolidate political power in Washington, D.C.).[5]

Since this idea is new to most of my readers, let us further demystify it by viewing it from the perspective of the American Revolutionary War. If Davis and his conservative Southern constituents (the Democrats of 1861) had been alive in 1775, they would have sided with George Washington and the American colonists, who sought to secede from the tyrannical government of Great Britain; if Lincoln and his Liberal Northern constituents (the Republicans of 1861) had been alive at that time, they would have sided with King George III and the English monarchy, who sought to maintain the American colonies as possessions of the British Empire. It is due to this very comparison that Southerners often refer to their secession as the Second Declaration of Independence and the "Civil War" as the Second American Revolutionary War.

Without a basic understanding of these facts, the American "Civil War" will forever remain incomprehensible. For a full discussion of this topic see my book, *Abraham Lincoln Was a Liberal, Jefferson Davis Was a Conservative: The Missing Key to Understanding the American Civil War*.

THE TERM "CIVIL WAR"

☞ As I heartily dislike the phrase "Civil War," its use throughout this book (as well as in my other works) is worthy of explanation.

Our entire modern literary system refers to the conflict of 1861 using the Northern term the "Civil War," whether we in the South like it or not. Of course, this is purposeful, for America's book industry,

The American "Civil War" was not a true civil war as Webster defines it: "A conflict between opposing groups of citizens of the *same* country." It was a fight between two individual countries; or to be more specific, two separate and constitutionally formed confederacies: the U.S.A. and the C.S.A.

which determines everything from how books are categorized and designed to how they are marketed and sold, is almost solely controlled by Liberals, socialists, globalists, and communists, individuals who will do anything to prevent the truth about Lincoln's War from coming out. An important aspect of this wholesale revisionism of American history is the use of the phrase "Civil War," which Yankee Liberals thrust into the public forum even as big government Left-winger Lincoln was diabolically tricking the Conservative South into firing the first shot at the Battle of Fort Sumter in April 1861.

The progressives' blatant American "Civil War" coverup continues to this day, one of the more overt results which pertains to how books are coded, indexed, and identified.[6] Thus, as all book searches by readers, libraries, and retail outlets are now performed online, and as all bookstores categorize works from or about this period under the heading "Civil War," honest book publishers and authors who deal with this particular topic have little choice but to use this deceptive term. If I were to refuse to use it, as some of my Southern colleagues have suggested, few people would ever find or read my books.

Add to this the fact that scarcely any non-Southerners have ever heard of the names we in the South use for the conflict, such as the "War for Southern Independence"—or my personal preference, "Lincoln's War." It only makes sense then to use the term "Civil War" in most commercial situations, distasteful though it is.

We should also bear in mind that while today educated persons, particularly educated Southerners, all share an abhorrence for the phrase "Civil War," it was not always so. Confederates who lived through and even fought in the conflict regularly used the term throughout the 1860s, and even long after. Among them were Confederate generals such as Nathan Bedford Forrest, Richard Taylor, and Joseph E. Johnston, not to mention the Confederacy's vice president, Alexander H. Stephens.

Confederate General James Longstreet was just one of many Southern officials who referred to the conflict of 1861 as the "Civil War."

In 1895 Confederate General James Longstreet wrote about his military experiences in a work subtitled, *Memoirs of the Civil War in America*, while in 1903 Confederate General John Brown Gordon entitled his autobiography, *Reminiscences of the Civil War*. Even the Confederacy's highest leader, President Jefferson Davis, used the term "Civil War,"[7] and in one case at least, as late as 1881—the year he wrote his brilliant exposition, *The Rise and Fall of the Confederate Government.*[8] Authors writing for *Confederate Veteran* magazine sometimes used the phrase well into the early 1900s,[9] and in 1898, at the Eighth Annual Meeting and Reunion of the United Confederate Veterans (the forerunner of today's Sons of Confederate Veterans), the following resolution was proposed: that from then on the Great War of 1861 was to be designated "the Civil War Between the States."[10]

A WORD ON EARLY AMERICAN MATERIAL

☞ In order to preserve the authentic historicity of the antebellum, bellum, and postbellum periods, I have retained the original spellings, formatting, and punctuation of the early Americans I quote. These include such items as British-English spellings, long-running paragraphs, obsolete words, and various literary devices peculiar to the time. Bracketed words within quotes are my additions and clarifications, while italicized words within quotes are (where indicated) my emphasis.

PRESENTISM

☞ As a historian I view *presentism* (judging the past according to present day mores and customs) as the enemy of authentic history. And this is precisely why the Left employs it in its ongoing war against traditional American, conservative, and Christian values. By looking at history through the lens of modern day beliefs, they are

Judging our ancestors by our own standards is unfair, unjust, misleading, and unethical.

able to distort, revise, and reshape the past into a false narrative that fits their ideological agenda: the liberalization *and* Northernization of America, the enlargement and further centralization of the national government, and total control of American political, economic, and social power, the same agenda that Lincoln championed.

This book rejects presentism and replaces it with what I call *historicalism*: judging our ancestors based on the values of their own time.

To get the most from this work the reader is invited to reject presentism as well. In this way—along with casting aside preconceived notions and the fake "history" churned out by our left-wing education system—the truth in this work will be most readily ascertained and absorbed.

CAPTIONS
☛ Most of the captions accompanying the monument images in this book were pieced together from original 19th- and early 20th-Century sources. As names and geographical boundaries can change over time, in some cases the originals may no longer match modern ones. The early information, however, preserves a piece of authentic Southern history.

LEARN MORE
☛ Lincoln's War on the American people and the Constitution can never be fully understood without a thorough knowledge of the South's perspective. As this book is only meant to be a brief introductory guide to these topics, one cannot hope to learn the complete story here. For those who are interested in additional material from Dixie's viewpoint, please see my comprehensive histories listed on pages 2 and 3.

INSCRIPTION ON A CONFEDERATE MONUMENT
Confederate soldiers were men whom power could not corrupt, whom death could not terrify, whom defeat could not dishonor.

Keep Your Body, Mind, & Spirit Vibrating at Their Highest Level

YOU CAN DO SO BY READING THE BOOKS OF

SEA RAVEN PRESS

There is nothing that will so perfectly keep your body, mind, and spirit in a healthy condition as to think wisely and positively. Hence you should not only read this book, but also the other books that we offer. They will quicken your physical, mental, and spiritual vibrations, enabling you to maintain a position in society as a healthy erudite person.

KEEP YOURSELF WELL-INFORMED!

The well-informed person is always at the head of the procession, while the ignorant, the lazy, and the unthoughtful hang onto the rear. If you are a Spiritual man or woman, do yourself a great favor: read Sea Raven Press books and stay well posted on the Truth. It is almost criminal for one to remain in ignorance while the opportunity to gain knowledge is open to all at a nominal price.

We invite you to visit our Webstore for a wide selection of wholesome, family-friendly, well-researched, educational books for all ages. You will be glad you did!

Five-Star Books & Gifts From the Heart of the American South

SeaRavenPress.com

INTRODUCTION

McGavock Confederate Cemetery, Franklin, Tennessee.

THERE ARE TWO primary reasons I wrote this book. The first is to furnish the facts about Lincoln's War for the everyday reader; facts that enemies of the South have being suppressing for 150 years. As there are thousands of anti-South books published every year for every one pro-South book, we can never have too many that provide the Truth—that is, Dixie's viewpoint.

Confederate monument, Montgomery, Alabama. Long may it stand.

This ties in with my second reason: to preserve as many images of our country's sacred Confederate monuments and memorials as possible for this and future generations. If we allow them to, South-haters will not only tear down every Confederate statue, they will also ban and destroy every image and description of them as well. In that event our descendants will never know that the U.S. was once generously dotted with thousands of beautiful Confederate memorials, South, North, East, and West. As a Southerner whose family goes back 16 generations to Jamestown, Virginia, this book is part of my own personal effort to ensure that this never happens.

If you are willing to make the same pledge, here is what you can do. Please share this book with family, friends, neighbors, and coworkers, and hand copies of it down to your children and grandchildren. You should know that our South-loathing foes—mainly uneducated, anti-American, self-deluded, radical Liberals, socialists, communists, and anarchists—labor tirelessly 24 hours a day, seven days a week using books, newspapers, magazines, TV, film, the Internet, and the pulpit to indoctrinate the world against the American South. If those of us who know the Truth are to reeducate people about Lincoln's War—so that Americans once again begin honoring Confederate soldiers and respecting their monuments—it will take every bit of fortitude, cooperation, ingenuity, and hard work we can muster to be successful.

Confederate Captain L. Y. Dean and his granddaughter Carolyn Dean Moore of Eufaula, Alabama. Dean lost his left arm at the Battle of Seven Pines, but would not desert his country, and so "fought to the end." Confederate soldiers like Capt. Dean did not make such sacrifices over slavery—an absurd notion by any standard—but for a principle. That principle was constitutional government, a Conservative idea that is part of what we now call Americanism.

Make no mistake. The "Civil War" continues. Let us honor our Confederate ancestors, Conservatives who fought for the "the grandest cause that ever rose, the purest that ever fell," by standing up to the intolerant and ill-informed Left. You can help eradicate what I call "Civil War illiteracy" by spreading the Truth about our valorous heroes in gray every chance you get. They will thank you in Heaven.

Lochlainn Seabrook
Nashville, Tennessee, USA
March 2018
In Nobis Regnat Christus

"LET HISTORY THAT LIVES TODAY NOT DIE TOMORROW;
PLANT IT DEEP IN THAT RICHEST SOIL: A CHILD'S HEART." — U.D.C. 1912

Section 1

UNCOVERING AUTHENTIC CIVIL WAR HISTORY

INSCRIPTION ON A CONFEDERATE MONUMENT

They fought for
the right of self–government.
Those who die for a right principle
do not die in vain.

Confederate President Jefferson Davis in 1867, shortly after being let out of prison. Since secession was legal (and still is), the U.S. government could not find a prosecuting attorney to try Davis in court. The false charge of "treason" was dropped, and the noble Conservative Southern leader was released.

1

THE TRUTH ABOUT THE CONFEDERATE SOLDIER

WHY SHOULD YOU and every other American honor the Confederate soldier and his monuments, as my subtitle enjoins? If you are familiar with authentic Southern history, you will already know the answer to this question. If you are in this category, this book will be a refreshing and welcome reminder. If you are one of those who does not understand why Confederate monuments are so important, why they are integral aspects of America's history, why they should be respected, this book will be a life-altering education.

THE MAJORITY OF AMERICANS WERE ONCE PRO-SOUTH
Today the phrase "Confederate monuments" stirs emotions ranging from joy and pride to sadness and anger. But from the perspective of history, both reactions cannot be correct, for the Old South was either righteous, patriotic, moral, and heroic, or she

was not. Only one viewpoint can be true.

If we go by the words of the anti-South movement, she was unrighteous, treasonous, immoral, and cowardly. However, the vast majority of people did not feel this way in April 1865 when General Lee laid down his arms at Appomattox, Virginia. Indeed, nearly all Southerners and at least half of the Northern population (the Conservative half) sided with Dixie. In other words, in 1861 at least 75 percent of Americans were pro-South, understood that secession was perfectly lawful, and supported Dixie in acting on her constitutional right to preserve self-government.

Why then are hate-filled anti-South notions so prevalent now? Where did they come from? Who invented them and why? And why do they continue to be embraced by so many today?

THE TRUE ENEMY OF THE U.S.A.

As I will demonstrate, the negative ideas which most Liberals and other South-haters associate with the Confederacy are not only wrong, they are the opposite of what the facts of history show. Indeed, if we use the definition of the U.S. as a constitutional confederate republic (which it has always been), then it was the North, not the South, who was the true enemy of America. For it was the Union which fought *against* the ideals of the Constitution and the intentions of the Founding Fathers. The South fought *for* the Constitution and the ideals of the Founders.

Confederate General Patrick R. Cleburne of Ireland.

THE VICTORS WRITE THE HISTORY

Not familiar with any of this? That is not surprising. For the past 150 years the truth has been buried under an avalanche of Left-wing mythology masquerading as "historical fact." After all, it is the victor's version of war that is accepted into mainstream history books, and the Liberal Yankee historians representing the winning side of the American Civil War—among the most vicious, deceptive, inhumane, amoral, biased, and unscrupulous men and women the world has ever known—have no intention of allowing you to know the truth about what went on between December 20, 1860 (the day the first Southern state seceded) and April 9, 1865 (the day the South withdrew from the field). Confederate General Patrick Ronayne Cleburne noted that losing the fight against the Northern aggressors

> means that the history of this heroic struggle will be written by the enemy; that our youth will be trained by Northern school teachers; will learn from Northern school books their version of the war; will be impressed by all the influences of history and education to regard our gallant dead as traitors, our maimed veterans as fit objects for derision.[11]

THE GREAT YANKEE COVERUP
To conceal this truth, the North invented what I call "The Great Yankee Coverup."[12] Authentic Civil War history was rewritten, revised, redacted, and suppressed during what Mrs. B. B. Ross, President of the Alabama Division of the U.D.C. in 1911, rightly called "the storm of hatred, misrepresentation, and slander which swept the country after the close of the Civil War."[13] Why bury the facts about the world's largest, most violent, and most needless internecine conflict?

It is because the truth would expose the illegality, the immorality, the duplicity, and the overt anti-American ideology behind the North's leftist actions. Simultaneously it would reveal the morality, patriotism, heroism, and righteousness of the Conservative Southern Cause. And what

American patriots Confederate veteran Rufus Hollis and his wife, circa late 1800s.

was that cause? It was *Americanism*, which Webster defines as an "attachment or allegiance to the traditions, interests, or ideals of the U.S.; the political principles and practices essential to American culture."[14]

AMERICANISM IS CONSERVATISM
Another word for Americanism is conservatism, and, as I will demonstrate, the Democrat Party of the Old South was the Conservative party of that era. The opposite of conservatism is liberalism, and, as I

will show, the Republican Party of the Old North was the Liberal party of that period. (Our two major political parties would not become the parties we know today until the all-important election of 1896.)[15]

THE VICTOR'S LIES HAVE GONE MAINSTREAM

The Great Yankee Coverup has been stunningly successful. Why? Because, 1) it has become part of America's accepted mainstream history, and as such, is taught in *all* of our schools, from kindergarten to college, and 2), it is being taught mainly by progressives, leftists, socialists, globalists, communists, and various other anti-American radicals, who are heavily invested in the idea of turning the U.S. into a socialist nation, the opposite of what the Founding Fathers intended.

To accomplish this goal, American socialists utilize traditional society-destroying methods, methods dating back to the beginning of the Civil War: they have completely revised, and thus falsified, authentic Civil War history; they continue to shame, degrade, slander, and humiliate the South, now through the mediums of TV, film, and the Internet; they practice the 150 year old custom of defacing Confederate graves, tearing down Confederate statues, removing Confederate monuments, banning the Confederate Flag, and, above all, inaccurately labeling the Southern people "racist" and "traitorous."

LIBERALS' ANGER IS OVER THEIR OWN LIES

Among the greatest of these invented lies is that the Confederate Battle Flag is "a symbol of racism, hatred, slavery, and treason." The ignorance behind this pseudohistorical imputation is breathtaking—and silly. When South-haters get upset over the sight of a Confederate Flag, their anger has nothing to do with reality. Their irritation is due to their own lie, a fallacy that they themselves fabricated! Needless to say, educated individuals do not engage in such behavior.

FAKE OUTRAGE, FAKE HISTORY

Naturally, Liberals have vindictively appended these same offensive labels to the South's Confederate officers and soldiers; and guilt by association has in turn attached them to these men's monuments, cemeteries, statues, busts, memorials, paintings, and gravestones. The result was predictable: widespread *fake moral outrage* over every Confederate image or symbol, aggressively reinforced by the Liberals' *fake history* concerning "Southern slavery," "Southern rebelliousness," and "Southern racism."

EXAMPLES OF THE MAINSTREAM'S FAKE HISTORY

That the American "Civil War" history taught in our schools, promoted on TV, advanced on the Internet, and portrayed in films is a pack of lies from beginning to end should not shock us. Nearly *all* of mainstream history is comprised of carefully manufactured frauds and untruths, nearly all of it invented by Liberals, the ones who benefit most from rewriting the past.

Take Mark Twain, Ralph Waldo Emerson, and Walt Whitman, as examples. All have been apotheosized, again, particularly by the Left, as American icons; as the epitome of the American ideal; as patriotic symbols of the archetypal American.[16] Much of this deification, however, is based on nothing but fake history, and the facts prove it.

☛ Twain—originally a "Confederate irregular" from Missouri who deserted and later transformed himself into a reconstructed "Connecticut Yankee"—was an academic socialist and anti-Catholic who detested the traditional Old South, backed organized labor and the labor movement, supported Liberal South-hating U.S. President James A. Garfield, referred to himself as a "revolutionist," preferred aristocracy to democracy, felt the federal government should be overthrown (for being *too* democratic), was ashamed of being an American, was against universal suffrage, believed that

Samuel Langhorne Clemens ("Mark Twain").

African-Americans were due reparations for black slavery (no mention of reparations for white slavery), proudly published the memoirs of Union hero Ulysses S. Grant, and associated himself with radical socialist Charles A. Dana.[17]

We will note here that Dana—a personal friend of both fellow socialist Horace Greeley (the owner and editor of the New York *Tribune*) and radical collectivist Karl Marx (the founder of modern communism)—was one of the many Left-wing revolutionaries who worked in the Lincoln administration.[18]

Ralph Waldo Emerson.

☛ Emerson, also a socialist,[19] deplored the South and the Southern people, and advocated war with Dixie in order to destroy what he called the "horrors of Southern slavery" (a Yankee myth if there ever was one). His hatred of the South was so intense that he favored secession as a means of ridding the U.S. of her, and once declared that Southerners who came North should be treated "like fanged animals." What Emerson meant by this exactly I will leave to the imagination of the reader. The bigoted New Englander, who seemed to dislike Lincoln simply because he was from Dixie (and hence referred to Old Abe as "the clown"), believed that Southerners are shiftless, lazy, shallow "fops"; good-for-nothing half-wits,[20] whom he described as "dumb," "unhappy," and "conceited."[21]

☛ Whitman was the author of the infamous book of poetry, *Leaves of Grass*, which many fellow Victorians considered indecent, immoral, tasteless, and even blasphemous.[22] They viewed the poet himself as an atheistic radical and an abominable libertine; a homosexual iconoclast who corrupted young men, promoted social anarchy, and eroded religious tradition. His wartime idol was Liberal Lincoln, with whom had much in common, most notably white supremacy. Both evinced an open disdain for African-Americans,

Walt Whitman.

whom they considered an "inferior race" that was unfit to marry European-Americans. Whitman, whose grandfather had owned slaves on Long Island, New York,[23] acknowledged his true feelings toward blacks, commenting: "I don't care for the niggers."[24]

Should any of these three men be considered ideal representatives of the United States of America? You may decide. It is safe to say, however, that if these facts were better known, the general public would demand that the names and images of Twain, Emerson, and Whitman be expunged from our history books.[25]

The same can be said for American Civil War history: if the public knew the facts, it would force the government to throw out all of America's school textbooks and write them from scratch.

WHY YOU SHOULD RESPECT CONFEDERATE MONUMENTS
With this knowledge at hand, let us now answer the question that I proposed earlier: why should every American honor the Confederate soldier and his memorials?

It is because he was fighting for America, Americanism, the Constitution, and the aims of the Founding Fathers: small government, limited government, self-government, and above all, states' rights. The Union soldier, on the other hand, fought against Americanism, his leader, Abraham Lincoln, even openly declaring war on the Constitution and states' rights by calling the Southern Confederacy an "illegal organization," and the constitutional right of secession an "ingenious sophism," an "insidious debauching of the public mind," and a "sugar coated invention" of the South.[26]

In the eyes of true Conservatives, this makes the Confederate soldier the ultimate 19th-Century American patriot!

THE FEDERAL GOVERNMENT VIEWS CONFEDERATE SOLDIERS AS U.S. MILITARY VETERANS
The U.S. government later acknowledged the truth about the Confederacy's servicemen by legally recognizing them as *U.S. military veterans*. This recognition began in the early 20th Century when Congress approved "U.S. Public Law 810" on February 26, 1929. Now updated as "Title 38, Veterans' Benefits, Amendment 2306," it reads:

Headstones, markers, and burial receptacles: (a) *The Secretary shall furnish, when requested, appropriate Government headstones or markers at the expense of the United States for the* unmarked graves of the following: . . . (3) *Soldiers of the* Union and *Confederate Armies of the Civil War*.[27]

On May 23, 1958, the idea of fully and legally Americanizing Confederate soldiers was made official when the U.S. Congress approved a regulation known as "Public Law 85-425." Though the last Confederate soldier died many decades ago, let us briefly review this act. The introduction reads:

To increase the monthly rates of pension payable to widows and former widows of deceased veterans of the Spanish-American War, Civil War, Indian War, and Mexican War, and *provide pensions to widows of veterans who served in the military or naval forces of the Confederate States of America during the Civil War*.[28]

Further on the act states:

Be it enacted by the Senate and House of Representatives of the *United States of America in Congress* assembled, That the Veterans' Benefits Act of 1957 (Public Law 85-56) is amended: [Clause] (e) For the purpose of this section, and section 433, *the term "veteran" includes a person who served in the military or naval forces of the Confederate States of America during the Civil War, and the term "active, military or naval service" includes active service in such forces*.[29]

According to Congress, as U.S. veterans, all former Confederate soldiers, sailors, and marines were to be paid a monthly pension in accord with U.S. law, as stipulated in Section 410:

Confederate Forces Veterans: The Administrator shall pay to each person who served in the military or naval forces of *the Confederate States of America during the Civil War* a monthly pension in the same amounts and subject to the same conditions *as would have been applicable to such person under the laws in effect on December 31, 1957, if his service in such forces had been service in the military or naval forces of the United States*.[30]

IT IS A CRIME TO DISTURB CONFEDERATE MEMORIALS

Thus, despite what Liberals, socialists, and the anti-South movement would like you to believe, according to no less than the U.S. Congress, *all* Confederate soldiers are indeed U.S. veterans (or more technically, are to be viewed as being the same as U.S. veterans).[31] This makes it a crime—one with a sizable fine and a prison sentence of up to 10 years—to move, violate, or even disturb a Confederate gravestone, statue, monument, or memorial of any kind. This is so important that I will repeat it: *according to U.S. Federal law it is a crime to move, violate, or even disturb a Confederate gravestone, statue, monument, or memorial of any kind.* It is actually a crime to even *attempt* to do any of these things.[32]

This statute, known as "18 U.S. Code 1369 - Destruction of Veterans' Memorials," reads:

(a) Whoever, in a circumstance described in subsection (b) below, *willfully injures or destroys, or attempts to injure or destroy, any structure, plaque, statue, or other monument on public property commemorating the service of any person or persons in the armed forces of the United States shall be fined under this title, imprisoned not more than 10 years, or both.*

(b) A circumstance described in this subsection is that

(1) in committing the offense described in subsection (a), the defendant travels or causes another to travel in interstate or foreign commerce, or uses the mail or an instrumentality of interstate or foreign commerce; or

(2) *the structure, plaque, statue, or other monument described in subsection (a) is located on property owned by, or under the jurisdiction of, the Federal Government.*[33]

To reemphasize, U.S. Public Law 85-425 states unequivocally that *"the term [U.S.] 'veteran' includes a person who served in the military or naval forces of the Confederate States of America during the Civil War."*

Many other laws come into play in the protection and preservation of the Confederate dead and their memorials. A partial list includes:

• The Antiquities Act of 1906 (16 U.S. Code 431-433).
• The Historic Sites Act of 1935 (49 Stat. 666; 16 U.S. Code 461-467).
• The National Historic Preservation Act of 1966 (49 U.S. Code 303).
• The National Environmental Policy Act of 1969 (42 U.S. Code 4321, 4331-4335).
• The Archaeological Resources Protection Act of 1979 (16 U.S. Code 469).
• In many states (e.g., West Virginia) Federal law strictly regulates:
"Protection of human skeletal remains, grave artifacts and grave markers; permits for excavation and removal; penalties; [this law] prohibits a person from *excavating, removing, destroying or disturbing any historic* or prehistoric *ruin, burial ground, archaeological site or human skeletal remains, unmarked grave, grave artifact or grave marker of historic significance without a valid permit."*[34]

Again, penalties are severe. Those who break such laws, including mayors and governors, must be held accountable—and authentic history is the witness that successfully prosecutes their crimes![35]

SEVENTY-SIX & SIXTY-ONE

Ye spirits of the glorious dead,
Ye watchers in the sky,
Who sought the patriot's crimson bed
With holy trust and high,
Come, lend your inspiration now,
Come, fire each Southern son
Who nobly fights for freeman's rights
And shouts for sixty-one.

Come, teach them how on hill, in glade,
Quick leaping from your side,
The lightning flash of sabers made
A red and flowing tide;
How well ye fought, how bravely fell
Beneath our burning sun;
And let the lyre in strains of fire
So speak of sixty-one.

There's many a grave in all the land
And many a crucifix
Which tells how that heroic band
Stood firm in seventy-six.
Ye heroes of the deathless past,
Your glorious race is run,
But from your dust springs freedom's trust
And blows for sixty-one.

We build our altars where you lie,
On many a verdant sod,
With sabers pointing to the sky
And sanctified to God.
The smoke shall rise from every pile
Till freedom's cause is won,
And every mouth throughout the South
Shall shout for sixty-one.[36]

JOHN W. OVERALL

2

THE TRUTH ABOUT LINCOLN'S WAR

THE CONFEDERATE SOLDIER'S official standing as a U.S.
military veteran and his unshakable patriotism and unwavering
devotion to the Constitution, are not the only reasons Americans
should honor him and his monuments, of course. The authentic history
of both the South and the War provide volumes of evidence that Dixie's
military men deserve the same respect, dignity, and admiration in death
as any other soldier who has worn one of the uniforms of America's
armed forces.

USING THE SCIENTIFIC METHOD TO STUDY LINCOLN'S WAR
In this chapter we will look at some of this history. We will approach
our topic using the scientific method; that is, we will rely on *historical fact*
rather than on *opinion, emotion, political correctness, presentism, and ideology*,
the nefarious techniques employed by enemies of the South. Only then
can genuine history be separated from fake history.

I will begin each entry with one of the thousands of lies that have
been invented by the anti-South movement, and I will answer it with the
truth—again, not based on my personal subjective views, but on the
objective testimony of Victorian Southerners (and in some cases,
Victorian Yankees), eyewitnesses who actually lived during and after the
War. The endnote at the close of each entry supplies the source where

the reader can learn more about that particular topic. Thus, importantly, we will be studying America's "Civil War" history *in context*—with all of its many nuanced shades of gray.

THE LEFT'S SIMPLISTIC APPROACH TO CIVIL WAR HISTORY

My methodology is in marked contrast to foes of the South; fact-haters who prefer a basic black and white approach when it comes to looking at our past. Why? The black-and-white, out-of-context, elementary school-styled history of the Left conveniently glosses over the many subtleties, particulars, and minutia that form the foundation of true history. And herein lies their purpose.

The Left uses heavily redacted, overly simplistic, out-of-context "Civil War" history to fool the public.

Their overly simplified conceptualization of Civil War history allows them to more easily suppress the facts; facts that are, in and of themselves, often each comprised of countless details—many of them requiring time, intelligence, diligent study, and perseverance to understand. Simultaneously, their crude "good guy (the Union) versus bad guy (the Confederacy)" approach has allowed them to thoroughly rewrite the chronicles of our ancestors to suit their ideological fantasies.[37]

It is clear that the scientific method used by Southern historians like myself is the only way to truly comprehend the full scope of Lincoln's War—precisely why it is rejected by the Left!

A CRASH COURSE IN AUTHENTIC "CIVIL WAR" HISTORY

Let us proceed now with our review of the genuine history of Lincoln's War, a massive suppressed body of material (derived mainly from official military reports, military histories, personal letters, and periodicals of the day) that—thanks to South-loathing revisionists—is utterly unknown to most Americans. This, in turn, will lay the foundation for the poignant pictorial of Confederate monuments that follows.

THE LIE: The phrase "Civil War" is the most proper name for the conflict, which is why Lincoln used it.

THE TRUTH: The phrase "Civil War" is the most improper name for the conflict, which is why Leftist Lincoln used it! It is, in fact, a deceptive term, intentionally created by enemies of the South for the sole purpose of misleading and confusing. And this is exactly what it has been doing for the past 150 years.

The true definition of a civil war was noted by Webster: "A civil war is a clash, struggle, or battle between opposing groups belonging to the *same* country."[38] The U.S.A. and the C.S.A., however, were two *separate* countries: the former founded as a constitutional confederacy in 1776, the latter founded as a constitutional confederacy in 1861.[39] Therefore calling the conflict the "Civil War" early on was a devilish Liberal ploy; a piece of Yankee propaganda meant to fool the world into thinking that the Union, being "indivisible," was, and would always remain, intact.

Why was this message so important to the Northern victors?

Because if, as Lincoln proposed, secession was illegal, then the South never officially seceded. This means it truly *was* a civil war and that the North's invasion of the South was both legal and justified. As this chapter will amply demonstrate, however, it was not legal, it was not justified, and it was not a civil war.[40]

THE LIE: Southerners are naturally rebellious, which is why they seceded.

THE TRUTH: Calling Confederate soldiers "rebels" and the conflict the "War of Rebellion" was one of the many clever tricks the North devised to conceal the facts, which are these: the South did not "rebel" by seceding any more than America's 13 original colonies "rebelled" when they seceded from Great Britain. In other words, if the War of 1861 was a "War of Rebellion," then the War of 1775 was a "War of Rebellion." If Jefferson Davis, Alexander H. Stephens, Robert E. Lee, and Stonewall Jackson were "rebels," then George Washington, Thomas Jefferson, Nathanael Greene, and Henry Knox were as well.[41]

And what is called the "rebellious" nature of Southern men and women is merely a Northern euphemism for Dixie's independent-mindedness. Southerners have always been more free-thinking and ruggedly individualistic than Yankees; more apt to go their own way, chart their own course, think for themselves. In the North, and among Liberals everywhere, one tends to find a monotonous intellectual conformity; an onerous and dreary group-think that the more free-wheeling Southerner sees as stifling, oppressive, and autocratic.

Though Confederate soldiers at first bristled at the nickname "rebels," they soon embraced it with a fervor as a way to taunt the North. For they were not rebelling against the U.S. government, as the Left falsely teaches. *They were rebelling against Liberal Northern tyranny!* Thus the name stuck and is sometimes still used by Southerners in its positive and true sense.

To repeat, however: one should never mistake the Yanks' once denigrating nickname for reality: the South did not "rebel" against the Union and the conflict was not a "War of Rebellion."

If C.S. President Jefferson Davis was a "rebel" and a "traitor," so was U.S. President George Washington.

THE LIE: The South seceded because she wanted to destroy then take over the Union.

THE TRUTH: The South never had a single intention, violent or even political, toward the Union. Our leader President Jefferson Davis was clear on this point:

> Actuated solely by the desire to preserve our own rights, and promote our own welfare, the separation by the Confederate States has been *marked by no aggression upon others, and followed by no domestic convulsion.*[42]

Far from wanting to take control of the Union, in reality the Southern states wanted nothing more than to separate from the Northern states as quickly as possible, and then be *left alone.* Here is how President Davis expressed it:

> *All we ask is to be let alone*—that those who never held power over us shall not now attempt our subjugation by arms. This we will, we must, resist to the direst extremity. The moment that this pretension is abandoned, the sword

will drop from our grasp, and we shall be ready to enter into treaties of amity and commerce that can not but be mutually beneficial. So long as this pretension is maintained, with a firm reliance on that Divine Power which covers with its protection the just cause, we must continue to struggle for our inherent right to freedom, independence, and self-government.[43]

For the South what was at stake was nothing less than the rights of the states as guaranteed by the Constitution, as Davis averred:

One of the incidents that led to our withdrawal from the Union was the apprehension that [under President Lincoln] *it was the intention of the United States Government to violate the constitutional right of each State to adopt and maintain, to reject or abolish slavery, as it pleased.*[44]

Let us note here that this statement is not about slavery, as anti-South partisans assert. It is about states' rights. Davis does not say that the South demanded the right to maintain slavery. He says that the Southern states demanded the right to decide for themselves whether or not to maintain or abolish slavery, a difference as wide as the Grand Canyon.

On slavery, as on many other issues, the South was *pro-choice*: let each state decide for themselves, she said. The North, however, was *no-*

So-called "Southern slavery" was nothing like the fantasy institution described in our history books. It was not even real slavery.

choice, which was unconstitutional—and herein lay the problem. Since the founding of the U.S. in 1776, the North had been slowly but surely taken greater and greater control of the federal government, and while doing so was incrementally undermining the Constitution. In the process, *the equal balance of power* between the Liberal North and the Conservative South (which many of the clauses in the Constitution were designed to help maintain) was gradually drifting northward, into the hands of South-hating progressives. Davis, a traditional Southern Conservative, articulated this growing problem as early as 1850, eleven years before the start of the War for Southern Independence. Said the then U.S. Mississippi Senator:

The danger is one of our own times, and it is that sectional division of the people which has created the necessity of looking to the question of *the balance of power*, and which carries with it, when disturbed, the danger of disunion.[45]

Southern writer Albert T. Bledsoe noted in 1907 that with the election of big government Liberal Abraham Lincoln November 6, 1860:

The balance of power was overthrown. The South lost, more and more, *her original equality in the Union*; and *the just design of the fathers was despised and trampled under foot by the Northern . . . [Liberals]*. Every census showed, that her power had diminished, as her dangers had increased; and *she no longer found herself in the original Union of equal sections. On the contrary, she found herself in a minority, which the Southern men of 1787 would have shunned as the plague*; and threatened by a vast majority as cruel as death, and as inexorable as the grave. *This was not the Union of the fathers; but the warped, and perverted Union of unjust [Liberal] rule and domination. The States of New England, never failed to threaten a dissolution of the Union [indeed, the Northern states seriously discussed secession numerous times before 1860], whenever, in their jealous imaginations, there seemed even a prospect that the balance of power might turn in favor of the South in only one branch of Congress.*[46] Yet the more this balance was actually turned in their favor, and the South, *contrary to the design of the fathers*, reduced to a hopeless minority, the more imperiously *they demanded her implicit submission to Northern rule, and the more fiercely was denounced here every struggle to maintain her original equality and independence as "Southern aggression."*[47]

At this point, the South had little choice but to separate: if confederalism—the Founders' experiment of a *voluntary* union[48]—was to continue, it was up to Dixie to take the reins; and this could only be done by secession. In 1863 President Davis gave the following explanation as to why the South left the Union:

The people of the [Southern] States now confederated became convinced that the Government of the United States had fallen into the hands of *a sectional majority [Northern Liberals]*, who would *pervert that most sacred of all trusts to the destruction of the [states'] rights which it was pledged to protect.* They [Southerners] believed that to remain longer in the Union would subject them to a continuance of a disparaging discrimination, submission to which would be inconsistent with their welfare, and intolerable to a proud people. They therefore determined to sever its bonds and establish a new Confederacy for themselves.

The experiment instituted by our revolutionary fathers, of a *voluntary Union of sovereign States* for the purposes specified in a solemn compact, *had been perverted by those [Liberals] who, feeling power and forgetting right, were determined to respect no law but their own will. The Government had ceased to answer the ends for which it was ordained and established.*

To save ourselves from a revolution which, in its silent but rapid progress, was about to place us under the despotism of numbers [majority rule], *and to preserve in spirit, as well as in form, a system of government* we believed to be peculiarly fitted to our condition, *and full of promise for mankind, we determined to make a new association, composed of States homogenous in interest, in policy, and in feeling.*

True to *our traditions of peace and our love of justice*, we sent commissioners to the United States to propose a fair and amicable settlement of all questions of public debt or property which might be in dispute. But the Government at Washington [i.e., Lincoln], *denying our right to self-government*, refused even to listen to any proposals for a peaceful separation. *Nothing was then left to do but to prepare for war.*[49]

Confederate General Stonewall Jackson.

Thus, Davis asserted, the South was forced to take up arms against the North, not over slavery, but

to vindicate the political rights, the freedom, equality, and State sovereignty which were the heritage purchased by the blood of our revolutionary sires.[50]

In 1911 a Southern woman articulated the secession of the Southern states this way:

We asked only for *that liberty that the constitution* drawn up among the colonies—newly free—*guaranteed to the States* taking part in the compact. We did not want to see sectionalism become king, and vassals made of weaker States. *We asked for equal State rights—and fought for them*, and planned to put the principle in effect among ourselves—and while our method failed through coercion, *our beliefs and opinions were so impressed upon the nation's life that we feel that a great victory was ours.*[51]

One of the primary barriers to understanding why the South fought is the false name originally given to the conflict by the victor: the "Civil War." But to misrepresent and mislead were, of course, the North's intentions from the beginning. Permanently settling this matter, in 1930, Miss Ida F. Powell, Chair of the United Daughters of the Confederacy Committee on the "War Between the States," wrote:

To combat error, and especially a historical error of long standing, is always difficult. It requires patience, tact, an absolute faith in the righteousness of our cause, *and yet a true understanding and a deep appreciation of the viewpoint of the other side.* Fortunately, time has assuaged the bitterness of past years. We should now be able to discuss dispassionately questions of history as they arise and to select the most accurate phraseology in describing events long since past; for a name given to a struggle and accepted as correct by both sides of that struggle defines its nature and determines the opinion of the world concerning it.

Such is the position we are taking in regard to the titanic struggle from 1861 to 1865, when, we maintain, that the conflict was not a "Civil" War, but was a "War between the States." *Each Southern State seceded from the Federal government after mature consideration, seceded with all the dignity and weight of their State governments and State; conventions back of them, and formed an independent constitutional government—the Confederate States of America.*

The South did not fight to overturn the Federal government. It did not wish to destroy that government and set up a rival administration in its place. The Southern States simply desired to withdraw peaceably from what had hitherto been considered a voluntary union of States, to leave the Northern States intact, with their recognized government untrammeled, and to form an independent government of their own. The South fought to repel invasion, to protect its homes and its inalienable rights as free men, and it was between two constitutionally organized governments that the war was waged.

If our Daughters of the Confederacy will remember these facts, if they will equip themselves with arguments to prove the justice of their cause when questions arise, if they will at all times use this phrase in referring to the struggle of the sixties—use it naturally, easily and as a matter of course, they will find that the combined action of over 60,000 earnest, loyal women will exert a wonderful influence over public opinion.

Our movement [the U.D.C. or United Daughters of the Confederacy] is distinctly *an educational movement. We must appeal to the thinking, educated classes, to those who mold public opinion.* Our Southern Divisions have the great mass of their people back of them. We [U.D.C. members], in the North, contend against great odds. But in every section of the country, tact, love, and the utmost fairness and consideration must be shown to the convictions of others.[52]

THE LIE: According to our country's pledge of allegiance, the Union is meant to be "one nation" and "indivisible." Therefore secession was wrong since it divided the nation.

THE TRUTH: The writer of the U.S. Pledge of Allegiance was a Yankee socialist named Francis Bellamy, whose views were the polar opposite of those of the Conservative Founding Fathers. Only socialists and uneducated Liberals continue to believe that we live in a "nation" and that it is "indivisible." Our "Pledge" was, in short, intended to be left-wing propaganda, as its author, its anti-American views, and its historical falsehoods clearly show.

As I demonstrate in the following entry, we are not a nation—a type of government in which there are no states' rights. We are a confederate republic—a type of government which is literally built on states' rights.

As for the Left's notion that secession is illegal because America is "indivisible," this is incorrect, and therefore must be called what it is: fake history. Confederacies and confederate republics, like the U.S.A., are by definition *voluntary* unions: a state may enter (accede) voluntarily and she may exit

Confederate Major Giles B. Cooke, the last surviving member of General Robert E. Lee's staff, proudly holding the Confederate Flag, circa 1929.

(secede) voluntarily. If this was not so, we would not be a republic, we would be a nation—a type of union the U.S. was not and is not, and was never intended to be.

In 1803 Southern judge, abolitionist, and lawyer St. George Tucker gave one of the most concise and accurate interpretations of the constitutional power of disunionization, that is, secession:

The Constitution of the United States, then, being that instrument by which the Federal Government hath been created, its powers defined and limited, and the duties and functions of its several departments prescribed, the Government, thus established, may be pronounced to be a *Confederate Republic*, composed of several *Independent and Sovereign Democratic States*, united for their common defence and security against foreign Nations, and for the purposes of harmony and mutual intercourse between each other; *each State retaining an entire liberty of exercising, as it thinks proper, all those parts of its Sovereignty which are not mentioned in the Constitution, or Act of Union, as parts that ought to be exercised in common.*

In becoming a member of the Federal Alliance, established between the American States by the Articles of Confederation, she [that is, a state] *expressly retained her Sovereignty and Independence. The constraints, put upon the exercise of that Sovereignty by those Articles, did not destroy its existence.*

The Federal Government, then, appears to be the organ through which the united Republics communicate with foreign Nations, and with each other. *Their submission to its operation is voluntary;* its councils, its engagements, its authority, are theirs, modified and united. Its Sovereignty is an emanation from theirs, not a flame, in which they have been consumed, nor a vortex, in which they are swallowed up. *Each is still a perfect State, still Sovereign, still independent, and still capable, should the occasion require, to resume the exercise of its functions, as such, in the most unlimited extent [that is, secede].*[53]

Let us note here that neither Lincoln or his war destroyed states' rights, like secession, as many today erroneously believe. It merely made them more difficult to act on under our ever growing, bloated, Big Brother government in Washington—with its over 600 departments and thousands upon thousands of intrusive federal laws. The Founding Fathers gave us what they called a "confederate republic," and it will continue to be a confederate republic well into the future—"if you can keep it," said the sagacious Benjamin Franklin.[54]

THE LIE: Secession was illegal in the 1860s, making the separation of the Southern states an act of treason.

THE TRUTH: Secession was legal in the 1860s, and still is. Here is why:

1) The U.S. was born out of secession (from Britain).
2) Secession, though not mentioned specifically in the Constitution (because both the Founders and the public considered it common knowledge, common sense, and common law), is tacitly protected by the Ninth and Tenth Amendments.
3) There is nothing in the Constitution prohibiting secession.

4) Without the right of secession the U.S. would be a nation, a type of government the Founding Fathers intentionally rejected. Instead they formed the U.S. as what they called a "confederacy," or more specifically, a "confederate republic," a type of political union in which the states may voluntarily enter and voluntarily leave at their own discretion.[55]

THE LIE: The South started the Civil War.
THE TRUTH: The North inaugurated the conflict when Lincoln diabolically tricked the South into firing the first shot at Fort Sumter. This fraud was well-known at the time, and Lincoln himself later acknowledged his role in it.[56]

President Jefferson Davis was certainly well aware of the North's deceitful shenanigans prior to the opening salvo of the War. In an 1864 interview with a Yankee journalist he stated emphatically:

> *I tried all in my power to avert this war. I saw it coming, and for twelve years I worked night and day to prevent it*, but I could not. *The North was mad and blind; it would not let us govern ourselves*, and so the war came, and now it must go on till the last man of this generation falls in his tracks, and his children seize his musket and fight our battle, unless you *acknowledge our right to self-government.*[57]

Jefferson Davis.

THE LIE: The North did not want war and did all it could to prevent it.
THE TRUTH: The opposite is true. Leftist Lincoln clearly desired war, for physically forcing the Conservative South back into the Union was, so he believed, the fastest way to stamp out states' rights—which were hampering his Liberal agenda. And what was that Liberal agenda? The installation of the anti-American concept of big government (known deceptively at the time as the "American System") in Washington, D.C. This, however, would have been impossible if states' rights were allowed to continue

subverting the Left's ultimate goal of enlarging the government and nationalizing the U.S.[58]

Meanwhile, Davis was sending one peace commission after another to Washington, D.C. in an attempt to stave off the bloodshed. Lincoln's response? He refused to meet with any of them. Instead, he called for 75,000 troops to immediately invade the South. The Left's most aggressive move toward obliterating the Conservative principle of states' rights was underway.[59]

THE LIE: The South fought to preserve slavery.

THE TRUTH: According to nearly every Southern leader, as well as the entire Southern populace, the Conservative South fought for her independence from what she rightly perceived as a dictatorial Liberal Northern government; her attempt to preserve both states' rights and the Constitution of the Founding Generation.[60] Here is what Confederate President Jefferson Davis said during the War in 1864:

> We are not fighting for slavery. We are fighting for Independence, and that, or extermination, we will have.[61]

Showing that the South's position never changed on this issue, here is what he said after the War:

> . . . [Slavery] never was an essential element. It was only a means of bringing other conflicting elements to an earlier culmination. . . . There are essential differences between the North and the South, that will, however this war may end, make them two nations.[62] . . . . The truth remains intact and incontrovertible, that the existence of African servitude was in no wise the cause of the conflict, but only an incident. In the later controversies that arose, however, its effect in operating as a lever upon the passions, prejudices, or sympathies of mankind, was so potent that it has been spread like a thick cloud over the whole horizon of historic truth.[63]

Davis' words are so important we will repeat them: "We are not fighting for slavery. We are fighting for independence."[64] Non-Southerners and South-haters who continue to claim otherwise are not only revealing their ignorance of the historical record, they are clearly displaying their disdain for historical facts. No one should learn, accept, or repeat history from such individuals.

THE LIE: The North fought to destroy slavery.
THE TRUTH: According to the majority of Northern leaders, the North fought to preserve the Union.[65] Here is what Union President Abraham Lincoln said:

> *My enemies* pretend I am now carrying on this war for the sole purpose of abolition. *So long as I am President, it shall be carried on for the sole purpose of restoring the Union.* . . . If there be those who would not save the Union unless they could at the same time destroy slavery, I do not agree with them. *My paramount object in this struggle is to save the Union, and is not either to save or to destroy slavery. If I could save the Union without freeing any slave I would do it.*[66]

An 1896 Republican Party campaign poster, featuring presidential candidate William McKinley (left) and vice presidential candidate Garret A. Hobart (right). It was during this election that the Democrats became Liberals and the Republicans became Conservatives, the parties we know today. Between 1854 and1896, however, the Democrats had been Conservatives and the Republicans had been Liberals. This political history has been carefully hidden from the public—until now.

THE LIE: Abraham Lincoln was a Republican, and therefore a Conservative.

THE TRUTH: The platforms of the two main parties were reversed in the 1860s, making the Republicans Liberals and the Democrats Conservatives. Lincoln was, in fact, a big government Liberal with socialistic leanings.[67]

THE LIE: Jefferson Davis was a Democrat, and therefore a Liberal.

THE TRUTH: Since the parties were the opposite of what they are today, the Democrats were the Conservative party of that era; which is why Confederate President Davis was a small government Conservative with libertarian leanings. The Republican Party would not become Conservative and the Democrat Party would not become Liberal, as they are today, until the election of 1896.[68]

THE LIE: The Civil War was a fight between the pro-slavery South and the anti-slavery North.

THE TRUTH: The North was not anti-slavery. *It was anti-slavery expansion.* Indeed, at the beginning of the conflict the official stance of both Lincoln and the Republican Party (the Liberals at that time) was not abolition, but rather the prevention of the spread of slavery outside the South. As for the Conservative South, she detested the institution of slavery and had been trying to rid her region of it since the mid 1600s.

Those who still believe that War was over slavery must ask themselves the following questions: what Northern man would be willing to risk his life for an outmoded institution that he cared little for, that had no effect on him personally, that existed primarily in a section of the country far removed from his own, and which he knew was going to be abolished sooner and or later?

And what Southern man would be willing to risk his life, along with his family, home, land, and entire town, to save an obsolete institution that he disliked, that he too knew would one day become extinct, that was not necessary to his region's economy, and that was only mainly practiced by a handful of wealthy individuals?[69]

The answer in both cases is a resounding "none." Clearly then, the fight was over something far more important, as the next entry shows.

THE LIE: The Civil War was a fight between the anti-American South and the pro-American North.

THE TRUTH: This is what the victors want you to believe, but nothing could be further from the truth. While both sides claim to be true patriots, they were fighting for opposing viewpoints: the Liberal North favored moving in the direction of a larger and more powerful national government—an idea that the Founding Fathers had earlier specifically rejected;[70] the Conservative South favored maintaining a small and limited central government, along with states' rights.

In the final analysis, our "Civil War" was nothing more or less than America's largest and most violent battle between conservatism (the South) and liberalism (the North).[71] At its core was the issue of how to interpret the Constitution regarding the powers of the central government and the powers of the individual states.[72] Thus in 1917 Leigh Robinson rightly called it a "strife between ideals facing in opposite directions,"[73] while Confederate General Robert E. Lee saw it as a "great struggle for constitutional freedom."[74] Neither side would compromise or accept the other's interpretation of constitutional freedom, and so "the war came."

Since the Confederacy was fighting for the self-governing ideals of the majority of the Founding Fathers while

Like every other Confederate authority, abolitionist Robert E. Lee asserted that the South fought not for slavery but for "constitutional freedom."

the Union was fighting against them, it is clear that it was the South who was acting patriotically, not the North. Thus the widely and correctly held view in Dixie has always been that

> coercion of the [Conservative] South was a conspiracy of unpatriotic [Northern Liberal] politicians to destroy the old constitution and blood-bought liberties of our country.[75]

Proof of this is Lincoln's notorious Gettysburg Address, which was nothing more than an adroit deception meant to cover up this fact. Of this infamous speech, H. L. Mencken said:

The Gettysburg speech was at once the shortest and the most famous oration in American history . . . the highest emotion reduced to a few poetical phrases. Lincoln himself never even remotely approached it. It is genuinely stupendous. But let us not forget that it is poetry, not logic; beauty, not sense. Think of the argument in it. Put it into the cold words of everyday. The doctrine is simply this: that the Union soldiers who died at Gettysburg sacrificed their lives to the cause of self-determination—that government of the people, by the people, for the people, should not perish from the earth. It is difficult to imagine anything more untrue. The Union soldiers in the battle actually fought against self-determination; it was the Confederates who fought for the right of their people to govern themselves.[76]

Naturally, anti-South historians ignore both the social reality and the true political history behind Southern secession and Dixie's defense of the Constitution. Despite this, one South-hater, Pennsylvanian James Gillespie Blaine, managed to come quite close to accurately (though sneeringly) describing the reasons for the unique patriotism of antebellum Southerners:

The Southern leaders occupied a commanding position. Those leaders *constituted a remarkable body of men.* Having before them the example of Jefferson, of Madison, of George Mason in Virginia, and of Nathaniel Macon in North Carolina, they gave deep study to the science of government. They were admirably trained as debaters, and *they became highly skilled in the management of parliamentary bodies. As a rule, they were highly educated*, some of them graduates of Northern colleges, a still larger number taking their degrees at Transylvania, in Kentucky, at Chapel Hill, in North Carolina, and at Mr. Jefferson's peculiar but admirable institution in Virginia. Their secluded modes of life on the plantation gave them leisure for reading and reflection. *They took pride in their libraries, pursued the law so far as it increased their equipment for a public career, and devoted themselves to political affairs with an absorbing ambition.* Their domestic relations imparted manners that were haughty and sometimes offensive; they were quick to take affront, and they not infrequently brought personal disputation into the discussion of public questions; but *they were, almost without exception, men of high integrity*, and they were especially and jealously careful of the public money. Too often ruinously lavish in their personal expenditures, *they believed in an economical government; and throughout*

James G. Blaine, a rare Yankee who understood the unique historical foundation of Southern patriotism.

the long period of their domination they guarded the treasury with rigid and unceasing vigilance against every attempt at extravagance and against every form of corruption.[77]

In other words, 19th-Century Southerners were political Conservatives, which naturally pitted them against the politically Liberal North. After 85 years of fending off the constant attacks and slander of their nosey, meddling, aggressive, self-righteous Yankee neighbors, is it any wonder that war erupted in 1861? Should anyone be surprised that in her last desperate attempt to preserve the Founders' original government and protect her people and property, the South finally decided to separate from a section of America that elected big government Liberal Abraham Lincoln; a left-wing ideologue who filled his administration and armies with radical socialists, and who threatened to overturn the Constitution and force the South back into an ever growing authoritarian Union—all at the tip of a gun barrel?

THE LIE: American slavery began in the South.
THE TRUTH: American slavery got its start in the North in 1638 when the slave ship *Desire*, from Boston, Massachusetts, brought back the first load of African slaves from the West Indies to New England.[78]

THE LIE: The American abolition movement was born in the North.
THE TRUTH: The American abolition movement was launched in the South in 1655, when a white Virginia

American slavery got its start in the North in the early 17th Century, when Yankees began importing Africans and legalizing slavery.

slave owner became the first American to voluntarily emancipate his slaves (at great financial loss, it should be added).[79]

THE LIE: The bulk of antebellum abolition societies existed in the North.
THE TRUTH: Throughout the entire history of American black slavery

(1638-1865), the majority of abolition societies existed in the South.[80]

THE LIE: Most early American abolitionists lived in the North.
THE TRUTH: We know this is false from the simple facts that American slavery started in the North and American abolition began in the South. Indeed, nearly all of early America's most famous and most influential abolitionists were from Dixie: George Washington, Thomas Jefferson, Patrick Henry, James Madison, St. George Tucker, James Monroe, and George Mason, to name just a few.[81]

THE LIE: All white Southerners owned slaves before the War.
THE TRUTH: As slavery was hated (and merely tolerated as a "necessary evil") throughout the South, as the South was the birthplace of the American abolition movement, and as slavery was an expensive institution, very few Southerners owned slaves. According to the 1860 U.S. Census, only 4.8 percent of white adult Southern men owned slaves that year (women and minors could not own "private property" at this time).[82]

THE LIE: All early American slave owners were white.
THE TRUTH: While less than 5 percent of white Southerners were slave owners, 25 percent of all free blacks were slave owners in early America—many who owned both black and white slaves. In some antebellum cities, such as Charleston, South Carolina, at least 75 percent of the town's free black population owned slaves.[83]

Contrary to Yankee myth, the Underground Railroad did little to help African-Americans and nothing at all to forward the cause of abolition.

THE LIE: The South always had more slaves than the North.
THE TRUTH: Since both the American slave trade and American slavery arose in the North, this is obviously not true. This certainly explains why, up until the late 1700s, the North possessed 60 percent of the 13 colony's slaves,[84] and why, during the early 1700s, 42 percent of all New York

households owned slaves, with the share of slaves in New York and New Jersey combined far exceeding that of North Carolina.[85]

THE LIE: The Underground Railroad saved hundreds of thousands of slaves.
THE TRUTH: The Underground Railroad was an inefficient and ineffective movement that, at most, helped around 2,000 slaves escape northward. And by "escape" I do not mean from the South, and by "northward" I do not mean that they ran to New England. The fact is that most of the slaves who used the Underground Railroad were Yankee slaves, not Southern ones, which is why when they fled, they went even further North, into Canada. The reasons for this are given in the next entry.[86]

THE LIE: The rules governing Northern slaves were humanitarian, gentle, and compassionate. The rules governing Southern slaves were barbaric, violent, and inhumane, with beatings, whippings, and torture being a "daily ritual."
THE TRUTH: As always, the opposite is true. From the very beginning Yankee slave laws were extremely harsh: African chattel were made slaves for life and brutal punishments—including branding, various tortures, hanging, and being burned at the stake—were handed out for even slight transgressions.

On the whole, relations between Southern white master and Southern black servant were friendly, sincere, respectful, and even loving.

In the far more tolerant Christian South, slave laws were quite lax and routinely ignored. The majority of Southern plantations were run by black managers and overseers, and Southern slaves were allowed to come and go as they pleased, visit friends and family on other farms, and take holidays, Sundays, and Saturday afternoons off. And unlike their Yankee counterparts, Southern slaves were paid a weekly salary, and, in exchange for their services, received "free" housing, clothing, food, and health care—*from cradle to grave.* Most significantly, *a Southern slave could purchase his or her freedom whenever they liked.*[87]

THE LIE: The white South began practicing slavery because her people were racists and loved enslaving people of color.

THE TRUTH: As discussed, as a whole, the humanitarian, abolitionist, Christian South never liked slavery; certainly never wished for it or attempted to "maintain it at all costs," as our Left-wing history books falsely preach.

In reality, after several generations, the founders of American slavery, Yankees, became disenchanted with the institution, and for a number of reasons. The North's short cool summers, long harsh winters, sandy soil, and hilly terrain made large-scale farming impossible and financially impractical. Along with this was the inevitable white racism that pervaded the Northern states at the time. Most Yankees found that they preferred living in an all-white region, completely separated from what they considered the "alien" culture of African-Americans.

Slavery was gradually abolished in the North, not due to humanitarian sentiment, but because of the region's short summers, hilly terrain, and entrenched white racism.

Not wanting to lose their financial investments in slavery, which amounted to billions of dollars, Yankee businessmen began gradually abolishing slavery in their region while simultaneously pushing the institution South, where the winters were short and the summers were long, and where the wide flat plains and alluvial delta lands provided the perfect environment for long-term, large-scale planting and harvesting. In this way, over the decades *Northern* slavery took root in the South.

It was not the choice of the South to became the home of slavery. It was foisted on her by crafty Yankee capitalists, who pretended to be abolitionists while continuing to profit from the institution. They were only stopped in their deviousness by the passage of the Thirteenth Amendment, which was ratified in December 1865, finally officially ending American slavery.[88]

THE LIE: The South practiced the worst type of slavery ever known in world history.

THE TRUTH: Actually, the South never practiced slavery. What it did practice was *involuntary servitude*, which is quite different than true slavery, in which a slave has virtually no rights. In involuntary servitude, however, slaves are protected by a myriad of human, religious, and civil laws, rights, and liberties. And, as noted above, along with these rights there come scores of privileges that are unknown to true slaves. This is why Southerners have always referred to their black chattel as "servants" rather than "slaves," the latter which is the more usual term in the North, where genuine slavery actually existed.

To find the world's worst and most inhumane forms of slavery, one must travel to Africa, which has been practicing authentic slavery on her own people for thousands of years. Here one will still discover primitive types of slavery that beggar description; savage forms of human bondage that never existed in the West.[89]

The world's most brutal forms of slavery have always been practiced in Africa—and still are. This Mandingo Chief has enslaved a fellow African to serve as his swordbearer.

THE LIE: Most Confederate soldiers and officers were slave owners. There were no slave owners among the Union soldiery.

THE TRUTH: The common Confederate soldier was not affluent enough to engage in the expensive business of slavery, and while a number of Confederate officers did indeed own slaves, most were humanitarian abolitionists who earnestly looked forward to the "day of Jubilee" (emancipation)—such as Confederate general and aid-de-camp to President Davis, James Chesnut Jr.[90]

Others from this group were famed Confederate Generals Robert E. Lee and Stonewall Jackson. Though the antebellum U.S. Census listed slaves in their households, neither were true slave owners in the literal or even civil sense. Lee, a non-slave owner who "hated slavery," was forced to adopt his wife's slaves when she inherited them from her parents. As soon as he was able, he freed them. Jackson, another non-slave owner, was considered so kindly that the slaves on neighboring farms asked to be purchased by him. After allowing them to pay off their indemnity, he freed them, and then built a church for black Virginians with his own money—a Sunday school at which he himself taught in his free time.

Two other celebrated Southern abolitionists of note were Confederate Generals Patrick Ronayne Cleburne and Nathan Bedford Forrest. Nearly a year and a half before the War ended, Cleburne, a native of Ireland, put forth the "Cleburne Memorial," which called for the enlistment of eligible black Southern men into the Confederate army and navy, along with full emancipation across the South.

Forrest, without question the most wrongly demonized Confederate soldier in history, closed down his slave business several years before the start of the War, then enlisted 45 of his servants after it began. He drafted 20 additional blacks from other residences as well, providing his famous cavalry with a total of 65 African-American soldiers. From out of these 65 black men, he hand-selected seven to serve as his personal armed bodyguards.

After the War most of Forrest's former servants eagerly returned to work for him, now as freemen. It was at this time that he called for repopulating the South with African immigrants (whom he considered superior workers) and publicly pledged his lifelong friendship to the black man and woman. Hardly the actions of a racist.

Mention now must be made of the many *Union* slave owners. In 1861, at the start of the War, there were still between 500,000 and 1 million slaves in the North, spread out among some 500,000 Yankee slave owners. A few of the more notable of these were General Winfield Scott, Admiral David G. Farragut, General George H. Thomas, and

Southern icon General Nathan Bedford Forrest, America's most misunderstood and wrongfully maligned Confederate soldier.

the family of Lincoln's wife, Mary Todd. The most infamous Union slave owner, however, was General Ulysses S. Grant, who kept his black chattel until he was forced to give them up due to the Thirteenth Amendment—enacted eight months after the War ended.[91] This is the same man who said that he would rather join the Confederacy than fight for abolition.[92]

Yankee soldiers admitted that there were not only countless slave owners in their ranks, but untold numbers of slaves as well. After the War, for example, John E. Rastall, a Union infantry officer, recorded the following:

> The First Regiment, Eastern Shore Maryland Volunteer Infantry, [U.S.A.] was organized at Cambridge, Dorchester County, Md., in the fall of 1861, and was commanded by James Wallace, Esq., an attorney at law and farmer. *He owned nine slaves, and had some of them in camp with him as servants.* Capt. John R. Keene, of Company C, *also had slaves with him, his father being the owner of about sixty. Other officers of this regiment had slaves in camp with them.*
> . . . *There were so many slaveholders in the command that the enlistment of their servants during the absence of the owners from home, and consequent loss of service, caused great dissatisfaction. The slaves of these loyal men,* who lost their property while away from home fighting for the Union, *were never paid for,* though a record of each slave is kept at the county seats of Eastern Maryland. *The [U.S.] government [under Lincoln] had agreed to respect the right of property in slaves on the part of owners who remained loyal to the Union . . .*[93]

Before launching yet another attack on Dixie over slavery, modern enemies of the South would do well to reread the last sentence—written by a *Union officer.* It calls into question, and exposes, every facet of the Liberals' fake Civil War history.

The casual Yankee acceptance of slavery noted in the above report is, no doubt, why, during the War, some Union troops not only allowed Mississippians to keep their black servants, but actually protected them as well.[94]

THE LIE: Yankee slave owners treated their slaves like family. Southern slave owners treated their slaves like animals.
THE TRUTH: As is nearly always true when it comes to the fake history invented by Liberals, the opposite is the case. Proof comes from the manner in which the two

Northern slave owner, Union General Ulysses S. Grant, said he would not fight for abolition.

sections dealt with the process of slave purchasing: Yankees registered their newly bought slaves on the same lists as their livestock, kitchen goods, and farming equipment. In contrast, Southerners registered their slaves as literal family members, and treated them as such.[95]

THE LIE: The South was a nation of slave traders.

THE TRUTH: The South never participated in the slave trade. This ignominious title must go to the North, the birthplace of not only American slavery (in 1638), but the American slave trade as well. This began in 1641, when Massachusetts became the first North American colony (state) to legalize slavery and monetize slaves.[96]

The facts are that all legal, and nearly all illegal, shipments of African slaves came to the U.S. aboard Yankee slave vessels, designed by Yankee engineers, constructed by Yankee shipbuilders, fitted out by Yankee riggers, piloted by Yankee ship captains, manned by Yankee crews, launched from Yankee marine ports, funded by Yankee businessmen, and supported by the Yankee population.[97]

In contrast, not only did the Southern Confederacy not engage in the slave trade (she did not own a single slave ship), but she banned the foreign slave trade in 1861, five years *before* the Union did.[98]

THE LIE: The Southern people could have ended slavery any time they chose, but they refused.

THE TRUTH: The South did not "refuse" to abolish slavery. *Like the North* (which never officially ended slavery, but instead gradually emancipated her slaves over a period of several hundred years),[99] *Southerners could not find a way to abolish the institution without harming both slave owners and slaves.*

For the former the issue was economics. Though nearly all Southerners deplored slavery (in particular slave owners, many who had involuntarily inherited servants from their parents), they had to consider their bank accounts: the average cost of a slave was the equivalent of $50,000 in today's currency. Large individual planters owned literally tens of millions of dollars in servants, while the total value of all 3,500,000 of Dixie's slaves in 1861 was the modern equivalent of $175 billion. Yet, the Confederate Treasury had less than $100 million in bank deposit and specie at the time; not anywhere near enough to compensate every slave owner without thoroughly bankrupting the brand new republic.

U.S. President Thomas Jefferson, one of our country's most brilliant minds, did not know how to end slavery without unleashing major social and economic upheaval.

As for the slaves themselves, while many were highly competent and intelligent individuals, the majority were uneducated and low-skilled. How could they survive being suddenly turned out into the streets after a lifetime of having every need provided and paid for by their owners?[100]

Abolitionist-slave owner President Thomas Jefferson perfectly summed up the intolerable situation this way: "We have the wolf by the ear, and we can neither hold him, nor safely let him go." The South, birthplace of the American abolition movement, was still struggling with this monumental problem when Lincoln invaded her borders in April 1861.[101]

THE LIE: The Confederate Flag is a symbol of racism, treason, and slavery.

THE TRUTH: The original Confederate Battle Flag was a *military flag* that was used by the Confederate army and navy between 1861 and 1865. For this reason alone it is obvious to all intelligent people that Dixie's sacred banner has nothing to do with "racism, treason, and slavery." But, some will counter, "it was used by a government that was racist and treasonous, and which practiced slavery, therefore its flag represents these things as well."

Unfortunately for South-loathers, this argument is also groundless, for the C.S. government was not built on, nor did it represent, white racism. Besides 8 million European Southerners, millions of non-white Southerners also supported the goals of the Confederacy, and many chose to join her armies in order to prove it.

The following is a conservative estimate of the numbers of the different races who served and fought under the Confederate Flag:

- 300,000 to 1 million African-Americans
- 70,000 Native-Americans
- 60,000 Latin-Americans
- 50,000 foreigners
- 12,000 Jewish-Americans
- 10,000 Asian-Americans[102]

Evidence for the black Confederate soldier specifically is widespread and abundant. In 1862, for example, former Northern slave Frederick Douglass wrote to Lincoln, trying to convince the bigoted president to allow black enlistment (an idea he had been resisting since the start of the War):

> *There are at the present moment, many colored men in the Confederate Army doing duty not only as cooks, servants and laborers, but as real soldiers, having muskets on their shoulders and bullets in their pockets,* ready to shoot down loyal [Yankee] troops, and *do all that soldiers may do* to destroy the Federal government and build up that of the traitors and rebels. *There were such soldiers at Manassas, and they are probably there still.* There is a negro in the [Confederate] army as well as in the fence, and our Government is likely to find it out before the war comes to an end. *That the negroes are numerous in the rebel army, and do for that army it heaviest work, is beyond question.*[103]

A Confederate soldier from Virginia noted that after the evacuation of Richmond, he came across a wagon train being guarded by heavily armed Confederate "negro soldiers":

> When within about one hundred yards of and in the rear of the wagon train, I observed some Union cavalry a short distance away on elevated ground forming to charge and the negro soldiers forming to meet the attack, which was met successfully, the Union cavalry retreating.[104]

Many more such examples could be cited.[105]

Concerning secession, as this was legal in the 1860s there was nothing "treasonous" about the South's separation from the Union.[106]

Finally, as to the charge that the Confederate Flag is a symbol of slavery, it is baseless, for, as we have seen, the South was the cradle of the American abolition movement and had been trying to rid her region of the institution for over 200 years.[107]

Contrary to vicious Yankee myths and erroneous Left-wing fairy tales, the Confederate Flag is actually a symbol of *racial inclusiveness*: her blue diagonal cross is none other than Saint Andrew's Cross (the national emblem of Scotland), her 13 white stars may be seen as representations of Jesus and the 12 Apostles, and her red field a mystical representation of the blood shed by our Savior. This makes the Confederate Battle Flag, not a symbol of hate or the white race, but a symbol of the human race, and of universal love[108]—the same doctrine taught by the Prince of Peace[109] and embraced by Southerners all the way back to Jamestown.

A photo the mainstream media does not want you to see: a group of courageous African-American Confederate veterans in 1910. A number of them are wearing medals, pins, ribbons, and various other awards and mementos from their arduous four-year long military service. The original caption writer correctly referred to these patriotic men as "faithful Confederates."

THE LIE: The Old South was racist.

THE TRUTH: Every section of the United States has had, and still has, its racists, North, South, East, and West. I include in this list, of course, black racists, brown racists, yellow racists, red racists, and white racists. But the South was never the "capitol of American racism," as South-haters and Liberals claim. It was the North, which even today hosts the headquarters of the modern Ku Klux Klan (not to be confused with the South's post Civil War KKK—which I call the Reconstruction KKK—and with which the modern organization has no connection).[110]

The severity of white racism in the American North was noted as far back as the early 1800s, when foreign visitors began commenting on the phenomenon. Their surprise was due to the fact that Yankees had been long telling them that American white racism existed only in the South. As foreign tourists were quick to discover, however, not only was there white racism in the North, it was far more entrenched and cruel than anything they had witnessed in the far more tolerant South. In the 1840s, for example, here is how one European, English writer James Silk Buckingham, described it: "The prejudice of colour is not nearly so strong in the South as in the North."[111]

Naturally, Southerners themselves were aware of the racist ruse, carefully constructed by Northern Liberals to shame the South and hide their own bigotry. Here, for instance, is how Robert Young Hayne, a South Carolina senator, described the treatment of free blacks living in the Northern states:

> . . . there does not exist on the face of the whole earth, a population so poor, so wretched, so vile, so loathsome, so utterly destitute of all the comforts, conveniences, and decencies of life, as the unfortunate blacks of Philadelphia, and New York and Boston. Liberty has been to them the greatest of calamities, the heaviest of curses. Sir, I have had some opportunities of making comparison between the condition of the free negroes of the North, and the slaves of the South, and the comparison has left not only an indelible impression of the superior advantages of the latter, but has gone far to reconcile me to slavery itself. Never have I felt so forcibly that touching description, "the foxes have holes, and the birds of the air have nests, but the Son of Man hath not where to lay his head," as when I have seen this unhappy race, naked and houseless, almost starving in the streets, and abandoned by all the world. Sir, I have seen, in the neighborhood of one of the most moral, religious and refined cities of the North, a family of free blacks driven to the caves of the rocks, and there obtaining a precarious subsistence from charity and plunder.[112]

THE LIE: The American South has always been inherently racist, which is why the Confederacy was racist, and it is why today's pro-South Confederate movement is inherently racist.

THE TRUTH: Thanks to the ignorant, the naive, and the brainwashed, who wrongly and unfairly use presentism to reinforce their falsehoods about the Old South, this blatant fallacy has been cluttering up the pages of our history books for nearly two centuries. Let us forever rid the world of it now.

When it comes to racism, we see what we want to see. Thus,

generally speaking:

1. Only racists see racism in everything.
2. Only racists see everything and everybody in terms of skin color.
3. Non-racists do not see racism unless it is overtly thrust upon them.
4. Non-racists judge others by their character, not the color of their skin.

Racists, in fact, invariably project their racism onto others; in particular, those who are not racist, a psychologically transparent, and thus futile, attempt to conceal their own racial bigotry. Indeed, it is plain that the most racist people and groups are the ones who cry "racism" the loudest and the most often. And since, as we have seen, the Liberal North has always been more racist than the Conservative South, early on the former transferred its racism onto the latter.

As this wartime photo of white Confederate soldier Andrew Martin Chandler (left) and black Confederate soldier Silas Martin (right) shows, the Confederate armies fought in racially integrated units, quite in contrast to the Union armies, which fought in racially segregated units.

If maleficent Liberals had not injected presentism into Southern history, this lie would have died a natural death long ago. Instead, it stuck, and so it has remained to this day, where it continues its role as one of the top sociopolitical weapons of the radical Left, the anti-South movement, and unenlightened Conservatives.

Yet, the truth—that Dixie has always been, and remains, the most racially tolerant section of the country—cannot be simply swept away, as many would like. By the standards of the Victorian Era, antebellum whites were not racist; certainly not any more than antebellum blacks, many who were revolted by the sight of white skin—a vestige of the native African belief that "only black skin is beautiful."[113] *The Old white*

South was only racist by the biased standards invented by the modern intolerant Left; history-ignorant presentists who use this fraud in their political "struggle" to socially "divide and conquer" the American people.

This villainous subterfuge has now been exposed for what it is, and it will be more fully revealed as my book unfolds.

THE LIE: Jefferson Davis was an anti-American secessionist, racist, criminal, and traitor who loved slavery and who arrogantly led the Southern states out of the Union.

THE TRUTH: Let us examine these points one at a time:

1) Like nearly all Southerners in 1860, Confederate President Davis was vehemently against the secession of the Southern states.[114] In fact, he only agreed to follow his state, Mississippi, out of the Union *after* she seceded on January 9, 1861.[115]

2) Davis adopted an orphaned black boy during the War, which he and his wife Varina cared for as their own child. Tragically, the youngster, named Jim Limber, was illegally and violently taken from the couple by the U.S. government after the War, never to be seen again.[116]

3) Davis detested slavery, but did not know, anymore than anyone else did, how to abolish the institution without ruining the lives of both slave owners and their servants. What he did do in November 1864, however, was to ask the Confederate Congress to allow the government to purchase 40,000 Southern slaves, with the intention of emancipating them after the War. Two months later, in January 1865, Davis asked Confederate Secretary of State Judah P.

Jefferson Davis and his second wife Varina (Howell) Davis before the War.

Benjamin to send Confederate commissioner Duncan F. Kenner to England to declare the South's commitment to full abolition. This was five years after the C.S.A. banned the foreign slave trade and nearly a year before the Union (U.S.) ratified the Thirteenth Amendment, which finally abolished slavery nationwide.[117]

4) Davis, a faithful Christian and an ardent Conservative, was one of the most incorruptible, law-abiding, upstanding men in American history, with a vigorous sense of morality and constitutional ethics. Indeed, a strong case could be made that had Davis been willing to violate national and international law (such as the Geneva Conventions) as Lincoln and his Yankee officers ordinarily did, the Confederacy would have been victorious.[118]

5) Since secession was legal in 1861 (just as it is today), Davis could not have been a "traitor." This fact was so clearly understood that after the War, as Davis sat in jail, the U.S. government was unable to find a prosecuting attorney willing to represent it in court. The case against Davis was widely regarded as unwinnable, which is why he was eventually freed without a trial or further punishment. Obviously, the "Civil War" was illegal and unjust from start to finish, and Lincoln and his administration had been well aware of it. But a war on the Conservative South benefitted the Liberal North, and it was on this heartless vindictive principle that it was waged.[119]

THE LIE: Abraham Lincoln was a law-abiding abolitionist who loved the Constitution and African-Americans, and who hated slavery and secession.

THE TRUTH: As we did with Davis, let us look at these one by one:

1) During the War Lincoln committed so many crimes that presidential and military scholars have yet to count them all. They number in the hundreds and include the following: completely subverting (and perverting) the Constitution; arresting and deporting Yankee anti-war advocates, like Ohio congressman Clement Laird Vallandigham who, though a civilian, was illegally tried by a military court; arbitrarily arresting and trying (by military commission) civilian draft resistors and others suspected of "disloyalty"; seizing rail and telegraph lines leading to the capital; suppressing and shutting down some 400 hundred pro-peace Northern newspapers—and arresting their owners; censoring telegraph communications; torturing both Northern soldiers (accused of desertion) and Northern citizens (accused of espousing anti-war

sentiment)—the preferred methods were "violent cold water torture" and being suspended by handcuffed wrists; illegally suspending the writ of *habeas corpus* across the entire U.S., and for the first time in U.S. history. The list is virtually endless.[120]

2) Lincoln was no abolitionist. He detested both abolitionists and the abolition movement, and said so on numerous occasions. Once when he was asked by a fellow Republican (the Liberal party at the time) how he felt about having abolitionists in his party, he replied that this was not a problem, "as long as I'm not tarred with the abolitionist brush."[121]

3) The U.S. Constitution is essentially a Conservative document, one that limits the growth and reach of the federal government while restricting the powers of the three governmental

The real Abraham Lincoln was nothing like the fabricated figure portrayed in our history books.

departments (executive, legislative, and judicial) and their members. This is why big government tax-and-spend Liberals like Lincoln disliked, and still dislike, the Constitution. This is why, in February 1861, Lincoln told New York businessman William E. Dodge that:

> I shall take an oath to the best of my ability to preserve, protect, and defend the Constitution. This is a great and solemn duty. With the support of the people and the assistance of the Almighty I shall undertake to perform it. I have full faith that I shall perform it. *It is not the Constitution as I would like to have it*, but as it is that is to be defended.[122]

Only a few years earlier he gave a speech in which he said that swearing to support the Constitution "is distasteful to me."[123]

4) If Lincoln loved the black race, one would be hard pressed to find evidence of the fact. What one discovers instead is a white supremacist, white racist, and white separatist who said that abolition was worse than slavery, who stalled the Emancipation

Proclamation for several years, was a member and leader in the American Colonization Society (whose goal was to "colonize" all African-Americans in foreign countries), who used slaves to complete the construction of the Capitol, implemented extreme racist military policies, used profits from Northern slavery to fund his War, often referred to blacks as "niggers" (both privately and publicly), said he was willing to sign the Corwin Amendment (which would have allowed American slavery to continue in perpetuity), campaigned until the last day of his life for black deportation, defended slave owners in court, and continually blocked black enlistment, black suffrage, and black citizenship.[124]

5) After being elected president, Lincoln claimed to be anti-secession. Indeed, according to him, "preserving the Union" was the one and only real reason he unlawfully invaded the South. But he had not always been against this all-important states' right. Here is what he said earlier, in 1848, about secession:

> *Any people anywhere, being inclined and having the power, have the right to rise up, and shake off the existing government, and form a new one that suits them better. This is a most valuable, a most sacred right—a right which, we hope and believe, is to liberate the world.* Nor is this right confined to cases in which the whole people of an existing government may choose to exercise it. *Any portion of such people that can may revolutionize, and make their own of so much of the territory as they inhabit.*[125]

Why change his mind in 1861? Liberal Lincoln grew more progressive over time, and eventually political expediency became more important to him than the Constitution. He was, in short, a virulent Left-wing propagandist and demagogue.[126]

THE LIE: Lincoln had nothing but good will toward the South, which is why he wanted to bring her back into the Union.

THE TRUTH: Like most other Yankee Liberals, Lincoln had nothing but ill will toward the South, which is why he once made the following comment to Interior Department official T. J. Barnett: "The entire South needs to be obliterated and replaced with new businessmen and new ideas."[127] It is why Southern poet Thomas Nelson Page held that the Liberal North had "intended that the [Conservative] South should be no more,"[128] it is why South-loathing Yankee Thaddeus Stevens declared that "the whole fabric of Southern society must be changed,"[129] and it is why, during the War, Yankee hero General William T. Sherman ordered his soldiers to take over and "colonize" the South.[130]

It is also why one of the first things the North did after the War was send thousands of Yankee school teachers into Dixie,[131] and it is why Ohio Liberal John Sherman asserted:

> We should not only brand the leading rebels with infamy, but the whole rebellion should wear the badge of the penitentiary, so that for this generation at least, no man who has taken part in it would dare to justify or palliate it.[132]

After the War, provincial, ill-tempered, South-loathing, New England Liberal-elitist, Representative Thaddeus Stevens, campaigned to severely punish Dixie for "rebelling" against the U.S. government. His vengeful plan included exterminating every trace of Southernness within her borders, including her military symbols and monuments. Stevens' vicious anti-South campaign continues today.

By his own admission, the real reason Lincoln went to war was money: he did not want to lose the "revenue" which the Southern states brought into the U.S. Treasury, for without the enormous taxes derived from Dixie he would not be able to pay for his big government Liberal agenda (the "American System").[133]

The South then was correct in her assessment that *jealousy* was at the root of the North's War on her. Wrote Confederate General Bradley Tyler Johnson:

> The habit of control and the practice of masterdom made the Southern man reliant, positive, and forceful. *He controlled the formative period of the new society. He formed the Union under the Constitution, and he directed the policy of the Union for the first seventy years of its existence. His power was the logical result of the institution by which he was formed. His whole energy was directed to the art of governing. The assertion of intellectual predominance and the exhibition of material power in the South produced irritation, envy, and ill will [in the North]. For thirty years prior to 1860 the North had been gradually making up its mind for the overthrow of the predominance in the South.*[134]

THE LIE: Lincoln's Emancipation Proclamation is America's greatest and most noble document, for it ended slavery by freeing the slaves.

THE TRUTH: Most Americans, North and South, white and black, who lived at the time would have heartily disagreed with this statement. As Lincoln was not an abolitionist, and was, in fact, a white racist/anti-abolitionist, whose party was founded in 1854 by Liberals and socialists to merely prevent the spread of slavery rather than end slavery itself, this statement rings false—because it is.[135]

What exposes the fraud is that Lincoln never once referred to his Emancipation Proclamation as a "civil rights measure" or even a "civil rights emancipation," which is what our Liberal, politically correct, mainstream history books claim it was. Instead, he always called it a "war measure" or a "military emancipation,"[136] for this is exactly what it was: an edict meant to free blacks, whose votes, it was hoped, would then help him get reelected in 1864, and who, in gratitude, it was assumed, would enlist in his armies to fill up the depleted ranks left by his rapidly dwindling white soldiery.[137] This cynical political use and abuse of minorities continues to be utilized by Liberals to this day.[138] Victorian Southerners easily saw through this Left-wing charade, rightly pronouncing it the Yankee's "pretended love for negroes."[139]

The hollowness of Lincoln's approach to emancipation is evident in a myriad of other ways as well. His Preliminary Emancipation Proclamation (September 22, 1862), for instance, contained a clause asking Congress to fund his plan to free the U.S. of blacks by deporting then colonizing them in foreign lands. Members of his administration convinced him to leave this clause out of the Final Emancipation Proclamation (issued January 1, 1863, and thus the version best known to the public) for fear of alienating abolitionists, whose votes he would need in the 1864 presidential election.[140]

This is the same man who declared that if a race war ever arose between whites and blacks, he would side with whites.[141] This is also the same white separatist who approved of a plan to put African-Americans in their own all-black state,[142] who publicly declared that "my first impulse would be to free all the slaves, and send them to Liberia [Africa],—to their own native land,"[143] and who, shortly before his election in 1860, announced to the world: "What I would most desire would be the separation of the white and black races."[144]

Lincoln's 1863 Final Emancipation Proclamation, sentimentalized in this chromolithograph from 1888, is one of the greatest frauds ever perpetuated by Liberals on the American public. Those who take the time to study it closely will be shocked by its many revelations. Among other things, it does not abolish slavery either in the North (where between 500,000 and 1 million slaves still existed) or in parts of the South captured and controlled by Union troops. These "excepted parts," the president's edict reads, are to be "left precisely as if this proclamation were not issued." Why did Lincoln choose to leave slavery untouched and intact across most of the country? He answers this question in the proclamation itself, calling it, not a "fit and necessary *civil rights* measure," but a "fit and necessary *war* measure," one that would terminate when the War ended.

THE LIE: Even if Lincoln was not always motivated for the right reasons, the abolitionist cause was just.

THE TRUTH: The humanitarian Christian South agreed then, and still agrees today, that abolishing slavery was always the right thing to do. This is, after all, why the American abolition movement got its start in the South!

What the South took issue with, and still takes issue with, is why the North began pushing abolition on her in the first place. This is hypocrisy of the most contemptible kind, for it was Northerners who founded the American slave trade, it was Northerners who founded American slavery, it was Northerners who benefitted most from these institutions, and it was Northerners who had the most to lose if both were abolished. Why then, in the early 1830s, did the North suddenly begin pretending that "slavery must be destroyed in the South"? Obviously it was not actually abolition Yankee Liberals had in mind, for in 1860 they were still reaping massive profits from slavery—and they continued to do so right through to the end of Lincoln's War. Indeed, it is well-known that Lincoln himself used profits from Northern slavery to fund his armies.[145] This is why New England abolitionist Lysander Spooner referred to Lincoln's "Wall Street boys" (Northern merchants and manufacturers involved in the Yankee slave trade) as

> lenders of blood money . . . accomplices of the slave-holders in perverting the government from the purposes of liberty and justice, to the greatest of crimes . . . accomplices for a purely pecuniary consideration, to wit, a control of the markets in the South.[146]

If the Yankee's meddlesome crusade to overturn slavery in the South was not about black civil rights or even true abolition, why then did they launch it? In two words: "social spite." Here is how a Southerner put it in 1919. The North's desire to force emancipation on the South, he wrote,

> was mainly the result of *social spite, springing from antipathy to the slaves as a race, and antipathy to the masters because they enjoyed a position impossible among northerners.* It was because of this basis in social sentiment, rather than in party creeds, that the [Yankee] antislavery movement had such indestructible vitality. This feeling was what made the [Liberal] North now profess to believe in the sacredness of a compromise when the Missouri Compromise was repealed, though they had said nothing of the kind when they broke the Tariff Compromise of 1833. This was what caused them with much self-confidence to declare that never again would a slave state be admitted into the Union, and to believe that they could indirectly practice state interposition against the fugitive slave law, and yet denounce it as treason and rebellion when tried openly by the South.[147]

By 1860 Conservative Dixie had been dealing with this type of Yankee interference, Left-wing vindictiveness, Northern jealousy, progressive doctrinairism, socialist political chicanery, New England South-loathing, and Liberal duplicity for some 80 years. Little wonder that on December 20 of that year the South decided that it had had enough. South Carolina took the first constitutional step toward resolving the problem by seceding. Five months later, "the war came."[148]

In the early 1890s President Lincoln's son, Liberal politician Robert Todd Lincoln, respectfully gave Confederate veterans permission to erect a Confederate monument in Chicago, Illinois. Due to both the complete rewriting and falsification of Civil War history and the spiteful demonization of the South, few if any Left-wing Yankees would follow Robert's example today.

THE LIE: There has never been a Confederate monument erected outside the South. The North would never allow it.

THE TRUTH: In the late 1800s, before Liberals had venomously revised Civil War history and taken over America's media, literature, and education systems, friendly relations still existed between many Southerners and many Yankees, even among former Confederate and Union soldiers. Thus, scores of Confederate monuments were raised in the North out of the innate respect which the Yankee then had for his former military rival.

One of the more notable examples of this occurred in Chicago, Illinois, where, with the approval and permission of Secretary of War under President James A. Garfield, Robert Todd Lincoln (President Lincoln's son), an enormous Confederate monument was dedicated on May 30, 1895. Some 100,000 people attended the ceremony, including scores of Union veterans and U.S. dignitaries.[149] Liberals, of course, do not want you to know these facts, which is why they have carefully excised them from our history books.

THE LIE: The South lost the Civil War, which means that God was on the side of the Union.

THE TRUTH: Few if any Southerners held this view in the Victorian

Era, and certainly even less of them hold it today. Many, like Lee, simply accepted the outcome as God's will rather than as God's preference for the North. What the vast majority of Southerners actually believe, however, is that *1) God does not take sides in human wars, and that 2) might always wins out over right, no matter what the initial cause is.*[150]

As the Union had nearly four times the men and military power of the South, not to mention unlimited funds,[151] this is the only explanation that makes sense to rational thinking people, and it is the one most widely accepted by unbiased military historians today. Otherwise, one is forced to explain why God, who animated America's Founding Fathers to begin with, would want the voluntary confederate republic and unique constitution they so carefully crafted under his inspiration on September 17, 1787, to be overthrown on April 9, 1865.[152]

THE LIE: The South is still obsessed, and will always be obsessed, with the War because she cannot forgive the North for winning.
THE TRUTH: The reverse is true. There is an old saying, one well steeped in psychology: "The injured one can always forgive, but he who maliciously wounds another can never forgive his victim."[153] This has always been true, and will always remain true.

THE LIE: The Union had nothing but respect for the defeated South immediately after the War.
THE TRUTH: So-called "Reconstruction" alone, which Southerners correctly saw as a second invasion of Dixie—a second war on the South, in fact, this one lasting 12 years (1865-1877) instead of four (1861-1865)—completely destroys this theory. In 1868, for instance, U.S. soldiers were seen guarding the burial spots of Confederate soldiers at Arlington Cemetery. Not out of respect, but to "prevent Southern ladies from placing flowers on their graves."[154]

For such outrages, and the countless other despicable crimes committed by the U.S. government during Reconstruction—many too horrendous to be described in a family-friendly book of this nature—I more accurately refer to this period as "Deconstruction."[155]

As we will see in our next chapter, however, by the 1890s the majority of Northerners and Union soldiers were seeking peace with the South, showering her Confederate soldiers with praise and honors.

THE LIE: The South could never have won the Civil War.

THE TRUTH: Not according to the Union's highest military official. In his 1885 memoirs, Yankee hero and U.S. President Ulysses S. Grant maintained that if the South had kept up the fight for just one more year, the Union would almost certainly have capitulated to Jefferson Davis' terms, the secession of the South would have been fully recognized, and the Confederate States of America would have been free to go to thrive in peace and prosperity.[156]

THE LIE: The Union won, proving that the North was right.

THE TRUTH: The historical facts prove without question, that as Samuel Augustus Steele said in 1914, *"the South was right."*[157] Based on the truths laid out in this book, you will never convince either genuine patriots or traditional Southerners of any other viewpoint. Facts will stand the test of time; opinions eventually fade away.[158]

Margaret "Maggie" Howell Davis Hayes, one of Confederate President Jefferson Davis' two daughters.

3

U.S. SUPPORT FOR CONFEDERATE SOLDIERS AND THEIR MONUMENTS

THE ANTI-SOUTH MOVEMENT is heavily indoctrinated, anti-intellectual, and ideologically driven. Thus, it is not surprising that its members continue to perpetuate the outworn myth that "the Confederate soldier was a traitor and a racist." As such, they deem Confederate soldiers unworthy of devotion and their monuments fit objects for scorn and immediate demolition. Based on this old canard, South-haters in turn went on to invent two of the greatest lies about Dixie and her courageous warriors:

1. No U.S. official, and in particular no Union officer, has ever venerated a Confederate soldier.
2. No U.S. government authority has ever donated money to the raising of a Confederate statue or attended the dedication of a Confederate memorial.

It is upon these flimsy fictions that they justify their irrational hatred of all things Confederate, including her servicemen and her monuments.

Let us now disprove these egregious misrepresentations once and for all, and be done with them. Nathan Bedford Forrest, for instance, wrongly abhorred by the uninformed today, was much admired by many of his Yankee foes during and after the War. Sherman, for one, was in awe of Forrest, declaring that the Confederate chieftain's tactics on the field "excited my imagination,"[159] maintaining that he was "the most remarkable man the Civil War produced on either side."[160]

Grant had similar feelings toward Stonewall Jackson, of whom he said:

> He was a gallant soldier and a Christian gentleman, and I can understand fully the admiration your people have for him.[161]

Our 26th commander-in-chief, President Theodore Roosevelt, maintained that not only were Confederate soldiers superior to Union soldiers, but that Confederate General Robert E. Lee was the greatest of all military officers among English-speaking peoples.

U.S. General Winfield Scott called Robert E. Lee "the greatest military genius in America," even offering him command of the United States army at the start of Lincoln's War (Lee turned him down).[162] Union General George Gordon Meade called Lee "by far the ablest Confederate general which the war produced,"[163] while the New York *World* awarded "him a place among the most eminent soldiers of history."[164] Union Colonel Charles Francis Adams Jr. noted that Lee's

> record and appearance during [his] final years are pleasant to dwell upon, for they reflect honor upon our American manhood.[165]

The New York *Herald* referred to Lee as "the Bayard of America," asserting:

> Never had mother a nobler son. In Robert E. Lee the military genius of America was developed to a greater extent than ever before.[166]

More recently President Trump's Chief of Staff, John Kelly, referred to Robert E. Lee as "an honorable man," a historical fact that will endure across Dixie as long as there are Southern states.

A number of U.S. presidents too have publicly declared their respect for the Confederacy and her soldiers. Theodore Roosevelt, for instance, stated that during the War Southern troops had been superior to Northern ones. Roosevelt made special mention of "the Old Rebel," Robert E. Lee, and his men. Said our 26th chief executive:

No man who is not willing to bear arms and to fight for his rights can give a good reason why he should be entitled to the privilege of living in a free community. *The decline of the militant spirit in the Northeast during the first half of this century [19th] was much to be regretted. To it is due more than to any other cause the undoubted average individual inferiority of the Northern compared with the Southern troops—at any rate, at the beginning of the great war of the rebellion [1861].*

The Southerners by their whole mode of living, their habits, their love of outdoor sports, kept up their warlike spirit, while in the North the so-called upper classes developed along the lines of a wealthy and bourgeois type, measuring everything by a mercantile standard (a peculiarly debasing one, if taken purely by itself), and submitting to be ruled in local affairs by low, foreign mobs, and in national affairs by their arrogant Southern kinsmen. The militant spirit of these last certainly stood them in good stead in the Civil War.

The world has never seen better soldiers than those who followed Lee, and their leader will undoubtedly rank, without any exception, as the very greatest of all the great captains that the English-speaking peoples have brought forth; and this although the last and chief of his antagonists may himself claim to stand as the full equal of Marlborough or Wellington.[167]

Left to right: William H. Taft, Warren G. Harding, Robert Todd Lincoln. All three men publicly honored the Confederacy and the Confederate soldier.

In 1917 our 28th president, political progressive Woodrow Wilson, attended a Confederate parade in front of the White House with his second wife, Edith Wilson.

President Wilson and his wife view a Confederate Reunion parade in Washington, D.C., in 1917. (Edith is in the center in a white dress and hat standing behind the rail; Wilson is to her left in the top hat.)

At Madison, Virginia, on August 17, 1929, Confederate veterans were invited to sit in the front row at the welcoming ceremonies for our 31st president, Conservative Herbert Clark Hoover.

Confederate vets waiting to greet President Herbert Hoover (not shown) in 1929.

Our 29th national leader, U.S. President Warren Gamaliel Harding, was also pleased to support the Old South and the Confederacy. In June 1922 he met with a group of Confederate veterans and their wives, then stood for photos with them outside the White House. As the veterans arrived for the meeting, the president's wife, Florence Harding, waved to them from one of the executive mansion's terraces.

U.S. President Warren G. Harding poses with a group of Confederate veterans and their wives at the White House in 1922.

President Harding's wife, Florence Harding, greets Confederate veterans and their wives arriving at the White House in 1922.

In December 1927 U.S. President Calvin Coolidge, our 30th chief executive, showed his respect for Confederate soldiers when he met with a group of Confederate veterans, then posed with them in front of the White House between two Confederate Battle Flags.[168]

President Calvin Coolidge stands reverently with Confederate veterans for a photograph on the White House lawn in the Winter of 1927.

In 1933, our 32nd president, socialistic Franklin Delano Roosevelt, happily met with Confederate veterans to accept their "allegiance."

FDR and Confederate veterans meeting in 1933.

At the beginning of the 20th Century, members of the United Daughters of the Confederacy petitioned the U.S. government for the raising of a Confederate monument at Arlington National Cemetery. On March 4, 1906, the appeal was approved by future U.S. president, then Secretary of War, William Howard Taft. At the laying of the cornerstone ceremony on November 12, 1912, Hilary Abner Herbert, secretary of the navy under President Grover Cleveland, gave a speech before a large Southern and Northern audience.

Other speakers included Nebraska Representative William Jennings Bryan and James A. Tanner, a former Union officer and head of the Union veterans organization. Taft, now U.S. president, gave a speech to the United Daughters of the Confederacy at a dinner held in the Daughters of the American Revolution's Centennial Hall.

Hilary Abner Herbert, U.S. Secretary of the Navy under President Grover Cleveland, addressing a huge crowd at the laying of the cornerstone of the Confederate Monument at Arlington National Cemetery, Arlington, Virginia, 1912.

A photo of a section of Ezekiel's famous Confederate Monument at Arlington National Cemetery that has been banished from our mainstream history books. Why? Because it shows an armed black Confederate soldier (center) proudly marching off to war, side by side with his white Southern brothers. Proof in stone of the African-American Confederate!

The dedication of the Confederate Monument at Arlington National Cemetery took place on June 4, 1914. Held the day after the 106th birthday of Confederate President Jefferson Davis, this was a truly gargantuan event, with thousands of both Confederate and Union veterans in attendance. Among the speakers was U.S. President Woodrow Wilson, who, despite being a progressive Liberal, was well versed in the authentic history of the South, and thus supported secession and Dixie's role in the War.[169]

The 32 foot Confederate Monument at Arlington National Cemetery was created by acclaimed sculptor Moses Ezekiel, one of the 12,000 Jews who fought under the Confederate Flag for the preservation of constitutional government. Naturally he included scenes on the memorial that he saw and experienced as a Confederate soldier, including a Rebel unit with a black Confederate soldier (see image left).

Ezekiel was later buried at the foot of his monument, along with three other Confederate soldiers: Captain John M. Hickey, General Marcus J. Wright, and Lieutenant Harry C. Marmaduke. On the rear of the base of the memorial there is an inscription by Confederate Chaplain, Reverend Randolph Harrison McKim, that reads: "Not for fame or reward, not for place or for rank, not lured by ambition or goaded by necessity, but in simple obedience to duty as they understood it, these men suffered all, sacrificed all, dared all and died."

What follows are more images showing the tremendous outpouring of support for Confederate soldiers by the U.S. government.

U.S. President Woodrow Wilson, a far left Liberal, speaking at the unveiling of the Confederate Monument, Arlington National Cemetery, Arlington, Virginia, 1914.

Another view of U.S. President Woodrow Wilson speaking at the unveiling of the Confederate Monument, Arlington National Cemetery, Arlington, Virginia, June 4, 1914.

Confederate General Bennett Henderson Young, speaking at the unveiling of the Confederate Monument, Arlington National Cemetery, Arlington, Virginia, June 4, 1914.

Another view of Confederate General Bennett Henderson Young, speaking at the unveiling of the Confederate Monument, Arlington National Cemetery, Arlington, Virginia, June 4, 1914.

Colonel Robert E. Lee, grandson of General Lee, speaking at the unveiling of the Confederate Monument, Arlington National Cemetery, Arlington, Virginia, June 4, 1914.

General Washington Gardner, Commander-in-Chief of the Grand Republican Army or G.A.R. (comprised of Union military veterans who served in Lincoln's War), speaking at the unveiling of the Confederate Monument, Arlington National Cemetery, Arlington, Virginia, June 4, 1914.

Mrs. Daisy McLaurin Stevens, President of the United Daughters of the Confederacy, speaking at the unveiling of the Confederate Monument, Arlington National Cemetery, Arlington, Virginia, June 4, 1914.

Mrs. Daisy McLaurin Stevens, President of the United Daughters of the Confederacy, at the unveiling of the Confederate Monument, Arlington National Cemetery, Arlington, Virginia, June 4, 1914.

Mrs. Daisy McLaurin Stevens, President of the United Daughters of the Confederacy, at the unveiling of the Confederate Monument, Arlington National Cemetery, Arlington, Virginia, June 4, 1914.

The actual unveiling of the Confederate Monument, Arlington National Cemetery, Arlington, Virginia, June 4, 1914.

The unveiling of the Confederate Monument, Arlington National Cemetery, Arlington, Virginia, June 4, 1914. Note the many U.S. Flags flying among the 13 Confederate Flags on poles surrounding the memorial.

U.S. President Warren G. Harding speaking at the Confederate Memorial Day gathering, Arlington National Cemetery, Arlington, Virginia, June-4-5, 1922. In the 1920s, before American Civil War history was revised and rewritten by Liberals, the Confederate Flag and the U.S. Flag were comfortably displayed side-by-side.

Another view of President Harding, Confederate Memorial Day, Arlington National Cemetery, June 4-5, 1922.

President Harding on the stand (back), Confederate Memorial Day ceremonies, Arlington National Cemetery, Arlington, Virginia, June 5, 1922.

U.D.C. members laying a wreath, Confederate Memorial Day services, Confederate Monument, Arlington National Cemetery, Arlington, Virginia, June 4, 1922.

United Daughters of the Confederacy holding the beautiful Confederate Third National Flag, Confederate Memorial Day, Confederate Monument, Arlington National Cemetery, Arlington, Virginia, June 4, 1922.

Confederate veterans, Confederate Memorial Day service, Confederate Monument, Arlington National Cemetery, Arlington, Virginia, June 4, 1922.

Another view of the unveiling of the Confederate Monument, Arlington National Cemetery, Arlington, Virginia, June 4, 1914.

What the foregoing proves without question is that the Confederate soldier was once considered a figure of not just Southern importance, but of *national* importance, a U.S. veteran, in fact; one who deserved to be celebrated, even lionized, and whose memorials commanded respect. Again, not just by Southerners, but by *all* Americans, whatever their home state, race, creed, or political persuasion.

Row of tombstones, Arlington National Cemetery, Arlington, Virginia, circa 1865.

The Left has recklessly suppressed these facts. Yet, this does not change reality: most Victorian Union veterans held their former Confederate foes in high regard, even contributing money to the raising of Confederate monuments, such as was the case with the beautiful Confederate monument in Franklin, Tennessee.[170]

What changed between the early 1900s and today? The Liberals' takeover of the media and the wanton redacting of our Civil War history, all part of the Left's nefarious plan to stamp out conservatism, suppress Christianity, trash the Constitution, further humiliate the South, normalize progressive policies, and take control of Washington.

INSCRIPTION ON A CONFEDERATE MONUMENT

We care not whence they came,
Dear is their lifeless clay!
Whether unknown or known to fame,
Their cause and country still the same,
They died—and they wore the gray.

WHY THE SOUTH SECEDED

"Not in hostility to others, not to injure any section of the country, not even for our own pecuniary benefit; but from the high and solemn motive of defending and protecting the rights we inherited and which it is our duty to transmit unshorn to our children."

JEFFERSON DAVIS, U.S. SENATE, JANUARY 21, 1861

The Confederate States of America

"No nation rose so fair,
Or fell so pure of crime."

INSCRIPTION ON A CONFEDERATE MONUMENT

This monument perpetuates the memory of those who,
True to the instincts of their birth,
Faithful to the teaching of their fathers,
Constant in their love for the state,
Died in the performance of their duty;
Who have glorified a fallen cause
By the simple manhood of their lives,
The patient endurance of suffering.
And the heroism of death;
And who, in the dark hours of imprisonment,
And the hopelessness of the hospital,
In the short, sharp agony of the field,
Found support and consolation in the belief
That at home they would not be forgotten.

Let the stranger who may in future times read this inscription,
Recognize that these were men
Whom power could not corrupt,
Whom death could not terrify,
Whom defeat could not dishonor.

And let their virtue plead for just judgment
Of the cause in which they perished;
Let the American of another generation remember
That the state taught them how to live and how to die,
And that from her broken fortunes
She has preserved for her children
The priceless treasures of their memories;
Teaching all who may claim the same birthright,
That truth, courage, and patriotism endureth forever.[171]

YEAR 1879

4

HONORING CONFEDERATE SOLDIERS AND THEIR MONUMENTS

FTER LEARNING THE truth about Lincoln's War and the Confederate soldier, only the most uneducated, uncivilized, mendacious, and unpatriotic will continue to criticize and defame him and the country he loved: the Southern Confederacy, patterned on the original Confederate States of America, the U.S.A.[172] Writing in the late 1800s, here is what one Southerner, Reverend R. C. Cave, had to say on this topic. Whether you sympathize with the South or the North:

> The heroic soul greets all [military] heroes as kindred spirits, whether they are found fighting by its side or leveling lance against it. It is the narrow, ungenerous, and selfish soul that can find nothing to admire in the courage, devotion, and heroism of its enemies.[173]

WHAT PRESIDENT MCKINLEY SAID
On December 14, 1898, at Atlanta, Georgia, with the bitter sentiment of the "Civil War" still lingering in the air, our 25th president, William McKinley, *a former Union soldier*, spoke for many Americans when he made the following remarks before a Southern group concerning both

Union *and* Confederate soldiers—many who were still alive at the time and sitting in the audience:

> Sectional lines no longer mar the map of the United States; sectional feeling no longer holds back the love we bear one another. Fraternity is the national anthem, sung by a chorus of forty-five States and our Territories at home and beyond the seas. The Union is once more the common altar of our love and loyalty, our devotion and sacrifice. . . .
>
> The old [U.S.] flag again waves over us in peace with new glories, which *your [Southern] sons and ours* have this year added to its sacred folds. What cause we have for rejoicing, saddened only by the fact that *so many of our brave men fell on the field, or sickened and died from hardship and exposure, and others returned bringing wounds and disease from which they will long suffer!*
>
> *The memory of the dead will be a precious legacy, and the disabled will be the nation's care.* A nation which cares for its disabled soldiers as we have always done will never lack defenders. *The national cemeteries for those who fell in battle* are proof that the dead are cared for, and the living have our love. What an army of silent sentinels we have; and with what loving care their graves are kept. *Every soldier's grave made during our unfortunate civil war* is a tribute to *American* valor.
>
> And while, when those graves were made, we differed widely about the future of this Government, these differences were long ago settled by the arbitrament of arms, and *the time has now come, in the evolution of sentiment and feeling, under the providence of God, when, in the spirit of fraternity, we should share with you in the care of the graves of the Confederate soldiers.*
>
> The cordial feeling now happily existing between the North and South prompts this gracious act, and if it needed further justification it is found in the gallant loyalty to the Union and the Flag so conspicuously shown in the year just past by the sons and grandsons of those heroic dead.
>
> What a glorious future awaits us if, unitedly, wisely, and bravely we face the new problems now pressing upon us, determined to solve them for right and humanity![174]

President William McKinley of Ohio, a former Union soldier, celebrated the Confederate soldier and his legacy, a shining example to all Americans.

Please note that President McKinley, a Yankee, asks his fellow Northerners, in fact *all Americans*, to share with Southerners "in the care of the graves of the Confederate soldiers." Were he alive today, the chief executive from the Buckeye State would be horrified to learn that other Northerners, and even many Southerners, are profaning, vandalizing, defacing, requesting the removal of, and even personally tearing down, the solemn monuments of Dixie's "brave men in gray."

A YANKEE ON CONFEDERATE HEROISM
Contrary to Yankee myth, in the decades following Lincoln's War most Union veterans evinced tremendous respect and even awe for the fearless Rebels who they had once faced across the battlefield. After all, since the South withstood a fighting force nearly four times its own size for four long years, the very term "Confederate soldier" became a synonym for courage in that day.[175] One of these Union veterans was William M. Armstrong who, in 1898, penned the following:

> *I heartily endorse everything that will bring us [Northerners] into closer friendship with the people of the South. I have an intense admiration for them*, and it's odd that this was first awakened during a fierce engagement. It was in Tennessee. Our men were stationed on a slope of ground behind parapets with head-logs. . . . Well, the only danger to which we could possibly be exposed during an attack was from our own batteries, which were so placed that they could fire over our heads. In such cases shells often burst before they reach their intended destination, and thus play havoc in the ranks they are meant to serve. Everything was against any who should attempt to come up that line, *but a force of Confederates tried it*. Their front lines were mowed down by the batteries, but on they came, as though they meant to take everything before them, until one could but wonder what madness possessed them. Again and again they were repulsed by merciless firing, but *every time they would reform and come marching back as proudly as if on review*, until—would you believe it?—they charged us seven times, and every time they came nearer, until in the last desperate assault our defenses were reached, and, clambering upon them, *they fought like madmen* with the butts of their guns until our batteries swept them down in a heap. *I never saw anything that could equal it in my life, and I have seen some thrilling sights. While they were fighting so heroically I felt like cheering them myself. It was such a*

Confederate supporter Miss Etta Hardeman, a Victorian Conservative and patriot from Georgia.

magnificent effort that, although victory was ours, it seemed trivial and mean because so easily won, especially when we watched the remnants of that gallant band fall slowly back, leaving the ground covered with gray-clad figures. Since then I have always thought that such foes would be worthy having as friends. I have made frequent visits in the South of late years, and have met many ex-Confederates, with whom delightful friendships were formed.[176]

If only today's Liberals were as benevolent and understanding toward the South as Yankee Armstrong, or President McKinley—a Union soldier who fought with the 23rd Ohio Infantry!

LEARNING & SHARING THE TRUTH

Victorian drawing of the Confederacy's four official flags: 1. The First National Confederate Flag; 2. The Confederate Battle Flag; 3. The Second National Confederate Flag; 4. The Third National Confederate Flag. All are still displayed proudly by patriots, even in foreign countries.

Let us close Section One with an appeal to each and every American. Those of you who know the South's true history and love and admire her people, have a responsibility to share your knowledge of and passion for Dixie with the rest of the world. It is understood that not everyone has the time, talent, funds, or health to march in protest rallies, go to Confederate events, print and hand out leaflets, write pro-South books and magazine articles, or attend city council meetings or court hearings. But everyone can do something, no matter how small, to help educate others as to the truth about the Confederate soldier and his monuments.

This would include everything from sharing educational pro-South posts on social media to talking with your family, neighbors, and coworkers about the Confederacy. This is important because if those of us who know the truth do not do what we can to preserve it, enemies of the truth will deride, ignore, suppress, and finally bury it, and the exceptional and awe-inspiring *true* history of both America and the American South will be lost. We owe this much to our descendants.

Those of you do not know the South's genuine history and who hate and malign her people, and in particular the Confederate soldier, also have a responsibility: as an American it is your obligation to educate yourself about our country's past, especially the period surrounding the War for Southern Independence. Not from the fake history found in books put out by Liberal-run university presses, or the fake history that fill our school textbooks—nearly all which are authored by malevolent anti-American Liberals and history-illiterate, discredited, South-hating organizations. Seek out sources that focus on fact rather than fiction; that base their information on genuine chronicles rather than on opinion, feelings, and abstract meaningless concepts like "social justice."

THE LIBERALS' SMEAR CAMPAIGN AGAINST DIXIE

It is one thing to disagree on politics. That is acceptable. What is not acceptable is to twist, bend, distort, and pervert history to suit one's personal sociopolitical ideology. Yet, this is one of the primary tools Liberals use in their efforts to undermine Americanism and erode Conservative values, as they prepare to instigate full-blown socialism.[177]

For us the most germane aspect of the progressives' plot to destroy traditional America is their outright war on all things Southern.

The Left's literary smear campaign against Dixie began in the late 1860s, when they began to rewrite our country's history to accord with their Alice-in-wonderland worldview, casting the North (Liberals) as the "good guys," and the South (Conservatives) as the "bad guys." This garbled, poorly written, confusing, purposefully misleading mess is what is being taught in our schools as "true Civil War history"!

Who could believe, for example, that nearly 3 million Yankees marched into Dixie in 1861 in order to slaughter their Southern cousins over slavery, an institution that the North had introduced to America to begin with, and which it was still practicing in 1861?[178] And who could believe that nearly 1 million

Confederate monument, Hemming Park, Jacksonville, Florida.

Southerners would take up arms to preserve an institution engaged in by less than 5 percent of their people, one that they themselves had been trying to eradicate since the mid 1600s, in the very section of the U.S. which gave birth to the American abolition movement?[179] And who would ever believe that the War was about "preserving the Union," when

the U.S. was created out of and built upon secession, a states' right tacitly guaranteed in the Constitution (Amendments Nine and Ten), and universally accepted by both the Founding Fathers and the American public well into the 1800s?[180]

As part of their program to divide and conquer using revisionist Civil War history, more recently Liberals and socialists have begun to label everything they do not like or agree with "racist." From here they have taken to verbally and physically attacking the objects of their hatred, which include all that is Confederate

The ill-informed like to compare Jefferson Davis to Adolf Hitler and Confederate soldiers to Nazi soldiers. The reverse is true: Davis and his soldiers were Right-wing Conservatives, Hitler and his soldiers were Left-wing socialists. Now you know why, in his autobiography, *Mein Kampf*, Hitler praised Lincoln's attempt to crush states' rights in the American South.

related: Confederate heroes, Confederate symbols, Confederate names, sacred Confederate sites, Confederate cemeteries, individual Confederate graves, Confederate statues, Confederate parks, Confederate artwork, Confederate memorials, Confederate monuments; anything associated with the Old South and her servicemen.

These are the identical tactics that have been, and still are, used by dictatorships, totalitarian states, and terrorist organizations the world over.

TRUE POLITICAL HISTORY
American Liberals, socialists, and communists like to define such political bodies as "Right-wing," while comparing the Confederate soldier with the Nazis of the 1940s. Many anti-South images on social media, for example, display the swastika and the Confederate Battle Flag side-by-side, as if they are related, or even one and the same. But this only reveals the depth of their ignorance of politics and political history.

Fascist authoritarians, like the Nazis, were *Left-wing*, and, in fact, Adolf Hitler, Joseph Stalin, and Benito Mussolini were all socialists of one kind or another, which lumps them in the same general pot of political stew as Bernie Sanders, Martin Luther King Jr., Fidel Castro, Che Guevara, Mao Zedong, Karl Marx, and Vladimir Lenin—of the thousands of radicals, revolutionaries, socialists, and communists that could be named.[181]

Traditional Conservatives, like Confederate soldiers, on the other hand, were *Right-wing*, for the two main political parties of that period were reversed: the Democrats of 1860 were Conservatives, the Republicans of 1860 were Liberals—a scenario that would not change until the election of 1896, when the parties we know today were created.[182]

Naturally, German socialist Karl Marx, the founder of modern communism, detested Conservative Jefferson Davis, but adored Liberal Abraham Lincoln, even sending him a congratulatory letter on his election, while simultaneously calling for war on the South. Lincoln later invited scores of leftist radicals into both his administration and his armies. One of these, socialist Charles A. Dana, his assistant secretary of war, was a personal friend of Marx.

THE CONFEDERATES FOUGHT FOR THE CONSERVATIVE IDEALS OF THE FOUNDERS

Our country was founded on Conservative principles, largely by Conservative individuals, who enshrined these principles in a Conservative-oriented document, the U.S. Constitution. In the War of 1861, the man who swore allegiance to these principles, to the Founding Fathers, and to the U.S. Constitution, was the Confederate soldier, a Conservative (a Democrat in that day). The man who fought against these principles, the Founding Fathers, and the U.S. Constitution, was the Union soldier, a Liberal (a Republican in that day).

Does this make the Yankee any less heroic, any less patriotic, any less courageous, than the Confederate? No, for he fought just as bravely and fiercely—and in many cases just as righteously—for his cause as the Southern enlistee did for his.

What it does mean is that in the great American war between

conservatism and liberalism, the Conservative Confederate soldier was closer to serving the Conservative ideals of the Founding Generation than the Liberal Union soldier. The Founders were primarily Conservatives with intensely Conservative values, who, after seceding from the tyranny of socialistic Great Britain, intentionally created the U.S. as a voluntary confederacy of "free and independent states"—even nicknaming it "The Confederate States of America." This is not Southern myth. It is American fact.[183]

This makes every American Conservative today a political descendant of the Confederate soldier, who stalwartly carried the banner of freedom for four long years against an intrepid but wrong-headed enemy: the Northern Liberal. For the Confederate soldier himself was a political descendant of

The Confederate Capitol in Montgomery, Alabama, on February 18, 1911, the 50th anniversary of the inauguration of Confederate President Jefferson Davis.

the Conservative Founding Generation: the latter fought for Conservative values in the first American Revolutionary War (1775); the former fought for Conservative values in the second American Revolutionary War (1861). And there it stands: historical truth!

CONFEDERALISM EQUALS CONSERVATISM

In summary, confederalism (a confederate government, like the C.S.A. and the original U.S.A.) is simply another word for Americanism, and Americanism is simply another word for conservatism—the political philosophy of the Founding Fathers. It is for this reason, if no other, that Confederate soldiers should be honored, celebrated, and respected, and their monuments should be protected, treasured, and venerated by all Americans for all time.

THE MEN WHO WORE THE GRAY

Oh, "The Men Who Wore the Gray,"
Oh, the men who dared the fray,
Upholding the grand principles for which our fathers fought;
Fame's resounding voice shall tell
How they strove and how they fell—
A monument of glory their high sacrifice hath wrought!

Let inspired pens portray
How these "Men Who Wore the Gray"
Came back, the struggle ended, every hope of justice fled;
All the future dark and void,
Maimed and poor, their homes destroyed.
Their wives and children weeping o'er the memories of their dead!

But affliction could not stay
Those brave "Men Who Wore the Gray"
From gathering up courageously their broken ends of life;
As they battled, so they worked—
Never yet had Southron shirked
The field where love and honor gave command to face the strife!

They are victors in that fray;
Now these "Men Who Wore the Gray"
Exult in their achievements for the land they love so well;
It has vanquished many foes—
It has blossomed like the rose—
The story of their proud success, its smiling homes can tell.

May God's mercy, day by day,
Bless "The Men Who Wore the Gray"—
Those fearless, peerless heroes, who waxed stronger as they strove;
While the people, heart and soul,
Grant to their decreasing roll
A Patriot's best recompense, the country's reverent love.[184]

AUTHOR UNKNOWN, 1895

INSCRIPTION ON A CONFEDERATE MONUMENT

Sacred to memory of Confederate soldiers
Who sleep in this cemetery
And to their surviving comrades who shall rest here.

Immortal heroes!
Your unparalleled courage, your blood, your patriotism,
Have bequeathed to all generations an example of sublime heroism,
And to your country an eternity of fame.

The confederacy, without an army, navy, or government, 600,000 volunteers sustained the assault of 2,778,304 men, supported by the strongest government in the world for four years. Its destruction rendered necessary a public debt of $2,708,393,885, the sacrifice of 349,944 lives and 1,366,443 pensioners.

Section 2

A PICTORIAL OF CONFEDERATE MONUMENTS

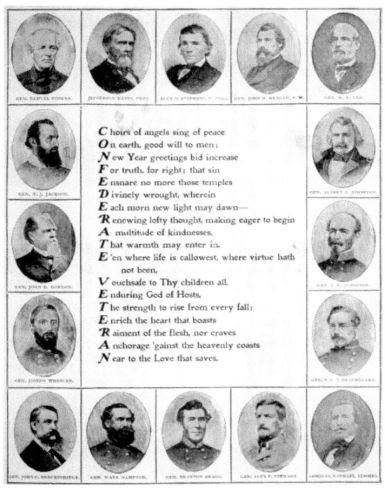

C hoirs of angels sing of peace
O n earth, good will to men;
N ew Year greetings bid increase
F or truth, for right; that sin
E nsnare no more those temples
D ivinely wrought, wherein
E ach morn new light may dawn—
R enewing lofty thought, making eager to begin
A multitude of kindnesses,
T hat warmth may enter in.
E 'en where life is callowest, where virtue hath
not been,
V ouchsafe to Thy children all.
E nduring God of Hosts,
T he strength to rise from every fall;
E nrich the heart that boasts
R aiment of the flesh, nor craves
A nchorage 'gainst the heavenly coasts
N ear to the Love that saves.

A Victorian acrostic poem, surrounded by sketches of some of the South's most beloved Confederate war heroes.

INTRODUCTION
to the Pictorial Section

REEDUCATING AMERICA AS TO THE
SOCIAL, HISTORICAL, & PATRIOTIC
IMPORTANCE OF CONFEDERATE MONUMENTS

Confederate monument, Paris, Texas.

T HE VAST MAJORITY of America's Confederate memorials were either inspired or raised (often both) by Southern women. In 1905 a Confederate veteran described them this way. They are "women of the true Southern type, who possess loyalty to the Southern cause and the fervor and zeal to memorialize the deeds of valor done in the historic sixties."[185] Their diligence encouraged ladies from other parts of the U.S. as well; not only from the Northern states, but even women from overseas. All spent years of their lives working industriously to preserve the memory of the Confederate soldier.

From the raising of funds and the hiring of artists, architects, sculptors, and metal workers, to casting, construction, and the unveiling, a typical Confederate monument took many years to complete, some as long as a decade or more. One monument I came across took over three decades to go from the day of inspiration to the day of dedication.

Not all Confederate monuments were created, paid for, and set up by Confederate individuals or groups. The U.S. government was behind the erection of scores of memorials dedicated to Confederate soldiers (which I have noted when possible). Sometimes businesses, companies, and corporations voluntarily engaged in Confederate monument building.   In one case, for example, a railroad company had a Confederate monument raised.[186]

In every instance, entire cities eagerly turned up for the dedication ceremonies, which hosted parades, festivities, song, food, and speeches. The cost in planning, time, money, creativity, energy, and love donated by the hundreds of thousands of individuals who participated in the building of our Confederate monuments (most which went up between the latter half of the 19th Century and the beginning of the 20th) is beyond reckoning.

Neither can anyone estimate the suffering and sacrifices of the Confederate soldiers who inspired them, many who sleep peacefully beneath these beautiful granite and marble memorials. Thus, it is an American tragedy of the most deplorable kind that the ignorant and dishonest are now able to have a Confederate monument taken down in only a matter of days without regard to, not only the history of the statues themselves, but the *authentic* American history behind them. As an educational tool, my book aims to change this situation.

BECOME PART OF THE PRO-CONFEDERATE MONUMENT MOVEMENT

Some of the memorials shown in the following pages are no longer in existence for one reason or another. Concerning those that have been removed, in particular by the bigoted, malicious, and uninformed, it is urged that my readers organize and campaign to have them returned and replaced—as was done successfully in Franklin, Ohio, recently.

If America takes down the statues of every individual that someone does not like or agree with, we will soon have no monuments left. History is history, for good or bad, for better or worse. It is time to accept history as it was instead of trying to rewrite it to match the ideology of the illiterate, the naive, the inculcated, the overly sensitive, and the politically motivated. There are countless statues across the U.S. of men and women that I do not like for one reason or another (Lincoln, Sherman, Grant, Sheridan, William Lloyd Garrison, Harriet Beecher Stowe, to name a few). But I do not want their monuments defaced or torn down. Let those who enjoy them keep them and honor them as they please. And let those of us who enjoy Confederate monuments keep them and honor them as we please. That is the American way.

CONFEDERATE MONUMENTS BELONG TO THE PEOPLE

In nearly all cases, early Confederate memorials were created and paid for either privately or by the American taxpayer—and at great expense: an average monument cost between $1,500 and $3,000 ($35,000 to $75,000 in today's currency); large ones cost far more (as much as $1 million by today's standards). Confederate monuments, stone symbols of the Southern soul (not to mention considerable time and money), belong to the people not the government.

Voting citizens get to decide on the monuments in their cities, not intolerant elitists, violent gangs, nescient bullies, and mob-rule. This tiny minority of individuals, blind with rage, hatred, bigotry, and ignorance, can no longer be permitted to control our towns.

UNION MONUMENTS IN THE SOUTH: UNDISTURBED

In contrast to all of this is the South, which generously permits Yankee

transplants, carpetbaggers, and scallywags to erect Union monuments nearly anywhere on her lands. Indeed, Yanks were raising monuments to their dead in Dixie even during the War, and all without resistance from Confederates. One of these is the Hazen Monument, dedicated and raised in 1863 to the memory of those Union soldiers who died at Stone's River, December 31, 1862. I know about this particular Federal memorial (located about two and half miles west of Murfreesboro) firsthand, because it is not far from my home here in Middle Tennessee.[187]

As the Conservative South permits the Liberal North to honor her Civil War soldiers both up North and here in Dixie, it is entirely justifiable for the South to expect the same courtesy in return.

The massive Hazen Monument (named after Yankee Gen. William Babcock Hazen) at Murfreesboro, Tennessee, one of scores of unmolested Union memorials in the South.

CONFEDERATE MONUMENTS: DATES & LOCATIONS

Dates accompanying my images are sometimes from obtuse sources, and so can indicate anything from when the monument was conceived or created to when it was erected or unveiled—and these could be months or even years apart. Where possible I include a monument's first location *as it was originally recorded by its Victorian contributor*, nearly always a non-historian (which opens up the possibility of errors).

THE ATTACK ON OUR MONUMENTS WILL NEVER STOP

No Confederate monument today is safe from the barbarous hordes of South-loathing progressives, nihilists, communists, and cultural Marxists. Waging an all out information war on Dixie, the Liberal's conformist group-think mentality is being used in Nazi-like fashion to historically cleanse all traces of the Old Conservative South from our schoolbooks and town squares. Along with this great whitewashing of American history, every artistic representation of anything even remotely related to the Confederacy, be it a painting, a bust, a gravestone, a plaque, or a statue, is being targeted for destruction.[188]

Racist hate groups masquerading as civil rights organizations, like the NAACP, are at the forefront of this un-American anti-South movement. If they would only take the time to learn the truth (as laid out in this book, and my many other titles), they would be helping us erect new Confederate monuments rather than seeking the destruction of the ones that already exist.

Actually, from 1867 (the probable year the first Confederate monument was raised) onward our Southern memorials have never been completely safe: the thuggish, fact-hating, anti-intellectual element of society known as the Left-wing, has been arrogantly meddling in the traditional South's affairs since the formation of the first U.S. confederacy in 1776. Indeed, this was one of the reasons war broke out between Conservative Southerners and Northern Liberals in 1861.

As I write these words thousands of Liberal South-haters, and even a few unschooled Conservatives, are sending letters to their city councils and local newspapers pushing to have the Confederate monuments in their towns taken down. Thus, every single Confederate statue still standing should be considered "endangered." This also includes Confederate monuments that have been erected outside the U.S.—for the history-ignorant bigot exists in all parts of the world.

Please use this book as inspiration to write your own letters, to make your own voice heard; form Confederate memorial preservation groups and use this book to defend the South, our heritage, our history, our monuments, and above all, the honor and dignity of our noble, bold, and patriotic Confederate dead. This is what our Victorian ancestors did, leaving us a sterling example to follow. We cannot and will not allow the suffering and deaths of America's Confederate military men to be in vain, and our many memorials to them will insure that this promise is kept and carried forward well into the future.

Rare photo of Confederate soldiers near the battlefield, Charleston, South Carolina, circa 1862.

I estimate that there are thousands, perhaps tens of thousands, of Confederate monuments in the U.S. alone, the expense of building and raising them amounting to well over $1 billion in today's currency. It would cost the modern taxpayer at least that much to tear them all down, a brazen fact that enemies of both the South and authentic history must take into consideration. But they were not just built at great financial cost. Confederate monuments were created out of an unquenchable love for liberty and truth. In eternal gratitude and humility, the educated, the compassionate, the honest, and the tolerant patriot will continue to view and maintain them in the same manner.

THE CANTING HYPOCRISY OF THE LEFT

While Liberal do-gooders, cultural Marxists, and the PC thought police busy themselves campaigning to remove *Confederate* monuments, they conveniently overlook the many politically incorrect *Union* monuments scattered over the U.S. They take down Forrest's monuments, for instance, because he was a slave owner. So was Grant. Yet his monuments are never touched. They take down Lee's monuments because he was allegedly a "racist." Totally untrue. Sherman, however, was an actual racist. Yet his monuments remain undisturbed. They take down Jefferson Davis' statues because he was supposedly a "traitor" to the U.S. Liberal Abraham Lincoln was the one who fought *against* the government and Constitution created by the Founding Fathers. Conservative Davis fought *for* them.

Lincoln also referred to blacks as "niggers," said he was against both interracial marriage and the creation of mulattos, advocated for U.S. apartheid, and spent his entire adult life trying to deport blacks in an effort to make America "white from coast to coast." Above all, he considered his race superior to all others—the true definition of racism. Despite these very public facts, one never sees Liberals trying to take down Lincoln's monuments.[189] Why?

Here in the South we call this "canting hypocrisy," for the manufactured hatred evinced toward Confederate monuments actually has nothing to do with racism, slavery, or treason. But it does have everything to do with the sociopolitical agenda of Liberals, socialists, and communists, along with their detestation of Western culture, Western history, and Western heritage. And no section in America represents the West's Conservative, Christian, Old European way of life like the traditional South, which is why their attacks on Dixie are so unremitting, vitriolic, and irrational.

WE WILL RAISE MORE CONFEDERATE MONUMENTS!

America is carpeted with countless thousands of Confederate memorials of all kinds, most in well-known places; but some were set up in remote, now lost, forgotten, or inaccessible areas. In any event, in a book this size it would be impossible to include them all. Those that I have included should be considered sacred representatives of the larger whole of the awe-inspiring statuary Americans (both South and North) have dedicated to the Confederate soldier over the past 150 years.

While periodically new Confederate monuments continue to go up (though far from the rapid pace of the Victorian Period), I predict that succeeding generations of patriots will found new Confederate monument associations, and that these groups will eventually raise thousands more Confederate memorials over our fair land. I am envisioning structures just as confidant, soulful, and magnificent as our Conservative 19th-Century ancestors designed and built.

It is my hope and prayer that this small volume will aid, inspire, and empower not only both current and future Confederate monument builders, but defenders of the Truth, as well—wherever they are from or whatever time period they live in. I wholeheartedly agree with my cousin, Conservative icon and C.S. President Jefferson Davis, who held that it is the living's solemn responsibility to memorialize

> those who gave all of earth to us and who could have looked forward to no other reward than securing to posterity the liberties to which we were born.[190]

And forever memorialize them we will!

Those who seek to stand in our way be forewarned. On the famed statue to the Unknown Confederate Dead at Oakland Cemetery, Atlanta, Georgia, the South portrayed herself as a sleeping lion. This was no accident.

L.S.

Why the South fought . . .

ATTENTION SOUTH-LOATHERS

There is an old Southern wives' tale that says a 13 year curse will befall any individual who treats a Confederate memorial of any kind disrespectfully. This would include those who deface, vandalize, or even campaign to take down Confederate memorials. (The number 13 comes from the 13 Southern states who seceded and formed our second Confederate States of America in 1861.)

Confederate monument, Alexandria, Virginia.

Most assume that old wives' tales are, by definition, false, and that curses are imaginary. But are they? Let the people who deface and assault our Confederate monuments test this theory for themselves.

ALABAMA

Confederate monument, Athens, Alabama, 1909.

Confederate monument, City Park, Birmingham, Alabama.

Confederate monument, Camden, Alabama, 1880.

Confederate and Spanish American War Monument, courthouse square, Carrollton, Alabama.

Confederate monument (right), Court House Square, Centreville, Alabama.

Closeup of the soldier on top of the Confederate monument (left), Florence, Alabama.

Confederate monument, Florence, Alabama, 1903.

Confederate monument, Gadsen, Alabama.

Confederate monument, Gainesville, Alabama, 1876.

Confederate monument, dedication, Greensboro, Alabama, May 12, 1904.

Confederate monument, town square, Huntsville, Alabama, 1905.

Dedication of the Confederate monument above, November 21, 1905, town square, Huntsville, Alabama.

Confederate monument, Courthouse Square, Jasper, Alabama, 1907.

Closeup of base of Confederate monument above, Courthouse Square, Jasper, Alabama.

Confederate monument, Livingston, Alabama, 1909.
It is 26.5 feet tall and weighs 40,000 pounds.

Cemetery at Confederate Memorial Park, Marbury, Alabama.

Confederate monument, to Confederate Admiral
Raphael Semmes, Mobile, Alabama.

Confederate monument, to Father Abram
Joseph Ryan, poet-priest of the Confederacy,
Ryan Park, Mobile, Alabama, 1913.

Confederate monument, Capitol grounds, Montgomery, Alabama, 1886.

The base of the previous Confederate monument, Montgomery, Alabama.

Battle scene on Confederate monument above, Montgomery, Alabama.

Closeup of Confederate soldier on previous Confederate monument, Montgomery, Alabama, 1886.

Confederate monument, to Confederate surgeon, soldier, and author John Allen Wyeth, State Capitol grounds, Montgomery, Alabama.

Confederate monument, Prattville, Alabama, 1908.

Old Live Oak Cemetery, the burial place of a number of Confederate soldiers, Selma, Alabama.

Confederate monument, Greenwood Cemetery, Tuscaloosa, Alabama, 1868.

Confederate monument, Tuscumbia, Alabama.

Confederate monument, town square, Tuskegee, Alabama.

INSCRIPTION ON A CONFEDERATE MONUMENT

The soldiers of the southern Confederacy
Fought valiantly for the
Liberty of state bequeathed them
By their forefathers of 1776.

"Who glorified their righteous cause and who made the
Sacrifice supreme in that they died to keep their country free."

Nor shall your glory be forgot
While fame her record keeps,
Or honor points the hallowed spot
Where valor proudly sleeps.
Tell it as you may,
It never can be told;
Sing it as you will,
It never can be sung—
The story of the glory
Of the men who wore the gray.

Confederate General Nathan Bedford Forrest's Guard of Honor from Troop A, Confederate veterans, 1914.

TO OUR SACRED CONFEDERATE DEAD

Go, scatter the flowers, one by one!
What are their names, and where are they from?
We know not, we care not—dead and unknown,
Without name or date to carve on the stone.

'Tis full enough for our hearts to know
They bravely faced and fought the foe;
Enough on each marble slab to say:
"A brother soldier who wore the gray."

They fought for a cause some say is "lost;"
But we, whose hearts fully know the cost.
Know that for us the cause hath shed
A glory and honor which hallows our dead.

On the living hath fallen their mantles of trust;
Immortal they reign, while we honor their dust.
'Tis a history now; 'twas a poem then,
All fraught with the glorious deeds of men.

Women and children sang the proud song
Which echoed our battle lines along
And floated on breezes from shore to shore—
Such grand achievements ne'er won before.

We honored and loved our soldiers then,
And crowned with laurel the bravest of men.
A history now, with unsullied page,
Hath been handed down to the present age;

And the deeds of the "boys who wore the gray"
Gives to our Southland a grandeur to-day—
Our hearts wildly throbbing with love and with pride,
As, shoulder to shoulder, we stand side by side.[191]

MRS. N. STEELE MOORE

ARKANSAS

Confederate monument, Austin, Arkansas, 1906.

Confederate monument, Batesville, Arkansas, 1907.

Confederate monument, Public Square, Bentonville, Arkansas, 1908.

Confederate monument, Greenwood Cemetery, Camden, Arkansas, 1886.

Confederate monument, to Confederate Col. Hiram L. Grinstead, Greenwood Cemetery, Camden, Arkansas, 1904.

Confederate monument, the city park, El Dorado, Arkansas, 1910.

Confederate monument, Fayetteville, Arkansas, 1897.

Confederate monument, Court House yard, Fort Smith, Arkansas, 1903.

Confederate monument, to the Confederate women of Arkansas, Capitol Grounds, Little Rock, Arkansas.

Confederate monument, Capitol building grounds, Little Rock, Arkansas, 1905.

Confederate monument, to the boy hero-martyr David Owen Dodd, grounds of the War Memorial Building, Little Rock, Arkansas, 1924. (The 17 year old was executed by Union soldiers after being captured carrying valuable Confederate documents.)

Confederate monument, Fairview Cemetery, Van Buren, Arkansas, 1899.

A CONFEDERATE OFFICER SPEAKS
TO A GROUP OF UNION VETERANS

Whatever may be the difference about the War and its causes, no brave or generous person can deny that it was made up of deeds of desperate valor, great military strategy, unparalleled endurance of hardship, and patriotic heroism on either side. You, my friends, felt that republican government and liberty itself were gone if the Union of the States were dissolved. *The Southern soldier believed in the sovereign rights of the States and the Union with only certain delegated powers and guaranteed rights, and defended his home and his property from invasion.*

The ardor with which both sides rallied around their respective flags and followed them through sacrifice, through danger and death, was equal, and proves their conscientious patriotism. Each soldier who laid down his life on either side for his country thought that he died for a holy cause. Both sides believed they were right. *Self-sacrifice unto death for what a man believes is heroism, and heroism that deserves immortality*—yes, more than deserves it: carries immortality in his breast.

It is given us now to see that high motives were not all ranged under one banner; that that sublime devotion that leads a man to leave wife and home and mother for the hardships of battle and the crown of death was displayed on both sides. *To underrate the courage, the endurance, and the heroism of the men who wore the gray is to dim the luster and tarnish the fame of the men who wore the blue.*[192]

CONFEDERATE MAJOR ALEXANDER BEAR, 1899

Young Confederate ladies of Lebanon, Tennessee, who represented the Southern states at the dedication of a Confederate monument there in 1899.

Confederate veteran Dr. Alexander Allen Faris of Hickman, Kentucky.

Miss Mary Kennon Jones of Gonzales, Texas, Confederate Maid of Honor for Texas at the Charleston U.C.V. Reunion in 1899.

CALIFORNIA

Confederate monument, Hollywood, California. Photo
captures the dedication of the first Confederate monument in
the West. It stands in Hollywood Cemetery and was unveiled
with "appropriate exercises" on June 6, 1925. Gen. W. C.
Harrison, commanding the Pacific Division, U.C.V., is to the
left, standing at salute.

A little Confederate miss in 1911, Elizabeth Cooper.

Confederate veterans, Florida, 1904.

ENGLAND

Bust of Confederate General Robert E. Lee, presented to the Royal Military College, Sandhurst, England, by the U.D.C., 1924.

The Confederate Battle Flag (far left) flying outside a home in England, early 1900s.

THE MULDOON MONUMENT CO.,

322, 324, 326, 328 GREEN STREET, LOUISVILLE, KY.

(OLDEST AND MOST RELIABLE HOUSE IN AMERICA.)

Have erected nine-tenths of the Confederate Monuments in the United States. These monuments cost from five to thirty thousand dollars. The following is a partial list of monuments they have erected. To see these monuments is to appreciate them.

Cynthiana, Ky.	Dalton, Ga.
Lexington, Ky.	Nashville, Tenn.
Louisville, Ky.	Columbia, Tenn.
Raleigh, N. C.	Shelbyville, Tenn.
J. C. Calhoun Sarcophagus,	Franklin, Tenn.
Charleston, S. C.	Kentucky State Monument,
Gen. Patrick R. Cleburne,	Chickamauga Park, Ga.
Helena, Ark.	Lynchburg, Va.
Helena, Ark.	Tennessee and North Caro-
Macon, Ga.	lina Monuments, Chicka-
Columbus, Ga.	mauga Park, Ga.
Thomasville, Ga.	Winchester, Va.
Sparta, Ga.	

When needing first-class, plain, or artistic work made from the finest quality of material, write them for designs and prices.

1905 magazine ad for the Muldoon Monument Co., Louisville, Kentucky.

Artistic representations of the Confederate soldier, 1905.

FLORIDA

Confederate monument, to the Confederate dead, Brooksville, Florida, 1916.

An attendant, UDC member Sister Esther Carlotta, writes of the dedication ceremonies:

This year one of our Chapters observed that day in a way that deserves special notice, for Brooksville Chapter, No. 71, dedicated its monument to the Confederate dead. Every organization of the city was out in force to honor the great event of the day, and hundreds of people came in from Tampa and other near-by places. Automobiles, decorated in Confederate colors and flying Confederate flags, formed a line of parade at the railroad station and, carrying Confederate veterans and the women of the sixties, led the way through the city. Nearly three thousand persons were in line, and the march swept on to the music of the Tampa Military Band until it reached the veiled monument.

Addresses of welcome followed from the city by Mr. C. M. Price and from the Brooksville Chapter by Mrs. Harry C. Mickler. After an address by Hon. F. L. Stringer, the son of a veteran, the Children of the Confederacy sang the official Division song, "Suwanee River."

Confederate monument, Hemming Park, Jacksonville, Florida.

Confederate monument, to the Confederate Women of Florida, Jacksonville, Florida.

Confederate monument, Marianna, Florida, 1923. This memorial commemorates the Battle of Marianna, September 27, 1864 (observed as "Marianna Day" by the Florida U.D.C.). Thousands turned out for the dedication on November 2, 1923. This monument is truly a national memorial: it was permitted and partially funded by the Florida State Legislature (American taxpayers), the dedication speech was given by Florida Governor Cary Augustus Hardee, the monument was presented to and accepted by the mayor, and the grand parade included the U.S. National Guard.

Confederate monument, Pensacola, Florida.

Veiled Confederate monument, The Plaza Park, St. Augustine, Florida, 1872.

Another view of the previous Confederate monument (without veils), The Plaza Park, St. Augustine, Florida (photo taken around 1891).

Confederate monument, courthouse lawn, Tampa, Florida.

A LAND WITHOUT RUINS

A land without ruins is a land without memories; a land without memories is a land without liberty. A land that wears a laurel crown may be fair to see; but twine a few sad cypress leaves around the brow of any land, and, be that land barren, beautiless, and bleak, it becomes lovely in its consecrated coronet of sorrow, and it wins the sympathy of the heart and of history. Crowns of roses fade; crowns of thorns endure. Calvaries and crucifixions take deepest hold of humanity; the triumphs of might are transient, they pass and are forgotten; the sufferings of the right are graven deepest on the chronicle of nations.[193]

FATHER ABRAM JOSEPH RYAN
NASHVILLE, TENNESSEE, 1878

Confederate General Samuel Gibbs French attacking the Union line at the Battle of Allatoona Pass, Georgia, October 5, 1864.

GEORGIA

Confederate monument, Albany, Georgia, 1901.

Confederate monument, to Confederate Major Henry Wirz, Andersonville, Georgia.

Confederate monument, Athens, Georgia.

Confederate monument, College Ave., Athens, Georgia, 1872.

Confederate monument, Oakland Cemetery, Atlanta, Georgia, 1874.

Confederate monument, the sleeping "Lion of the South," to the Unknown Confederate Dead, Oakland Cemetery, Atlanta, Georgia.

TO THE UNKNOWN CONFEDERATE DEAD

Extract from a speech delivered by Confederate General
Samuel Gibbs French, Orlando, Florida, June 3, 1893.

When the war ended, the Federal government, with commendable zeal, very humanely collected most of its dead and had their remains removed to its beautiful cemeteries, and there keeps green the sod and fresh the flowers on their graves. There was no Confederate government to collect and care for the remains of the Confederate dead. Along the banks of the "Father of Waters" for more than a thousand miles the inhabitants tread unawares over the unknown graves of those who battled for the South. Along the shores of the Potomac, the Rappahannock, and the James wave the golden harvests on soil enriched by their blood and moldering dust. There the grapes grow more luscious and the wine is redder.

From the capes of the Chesapeake adown the stormy Atlantic, and trending around the Gulf, rest thousands of our dead; or go to the heights of Allatoona, to Lookout's lofty peak, or Kennesaw Mountain's top, and you may seek in vain where the dead rest. Time, with the relentless force of the elements, has obliterated all traces of their graves from human eye; they are known only to Him who can tell where Moses sleeps in "a vale in the land of Moab."

So the forgotten are not forgot, the Hand that made the thunder's home comes down every spring and paints with bright colors the little wild flowers that grow over their resting places, and they are bright on Decoration Day. The rosy morn announces first to them that the night is gone, and when the day is past and the landscape veiled with evening's shade, high on the mountain top the last ray of the setting sun lovingly lingers longest, loath to leave the lonely place where the bright-eyed children of the Confederacy rest in death. And wherefore did they die?

They fell in defense of their homes, their families, their country, and those civil rights arising from that liberty God gave man as a heritage in the beginning. They furnished to their country much that will be noble in history, wonderful in story, tender in song, and a large share of that glory which will claim the admiration of mankind. We can to day place no wreaths of immortelles on their unknown graves, yet we can rest assured that the echoes of posterity will render their deeds illustrious.

And now, as I look back on the past and recall to mind your trials and sufferings—which will be forgotten—I am sure the world will not forget that your valor merited a success which is better now than to have achieved it.[194]

Confederate monument, to Confederate
General John Brown Gordon, Atlanta,
Georgia.

Monument to Confederate
Senator Benjamin Harvey Hill,
Atlanta, Georgia.

Confederate General William Henry Talbot Walker.

Confederate monument, to Confederate Gen. William Henry Talbot Walker, Atlanta, Georgia.

Confederate monument, Broad St., Augusta, Georgia, 1878.

Confederate monument, Courthouse, Calhoun, Georgia.

Note: What was known by many Victorian Southerners as "Chickamauga National Military Park" is actually called "Chickamauga and Chattanooga National Military Park." Established in 1895, it straddles the Tennessee-Georgia state line, covering two major points of interest: Chickamauga Battlefield in Georgia, and Lookout Mountain Battlefield in Tennessee. The park's headquarters are at Fort Oglethorpe, Georgia, however, so I have listed its Confederate monuments under the Peach State.

Confederate monument, to Georgia's Confederate dead, Poe field, Chickamauga National Military Park, Georgia/Tennessee, 1899.

Confederate monument, to Kentucky's Confederate dead, Chickamauga National Military Park, Georgia/Tennessee.

Confederate monument, to Joe L. Campbell, Confederate color bearer, First Tennessee Infantry, Chickamauga National Military Park, Georgia/Tennessee.

Confederate monument, to Alabama's Confederate soldiers, Chickamauga National Military Park, Georgia/Tennessee, 1913.

Confederate monument, to South Carolina's Confederate soldiers, Chickamauga National Military Park, Georgia/Tennessee.

Confederate monument, to Tennessee's Confederate soldiers who fought at the Battle of Chickamauga, Chickamauga National Military Park, Georgia/Tennessee.

Another view of the Confederate monument above, Chickamauga National Military Park, Georgia/Tennessee.

Confederate monument, Central Park, Covington, Georgia, 1906.

Confederate cemetery, Covington, Georgia.

Confederate monument, to Confederate Vice President and Georgia statesman Alexander H. Stephens, "Liberty Hall" (Stephens' home), Crawfordsville, Georgia, 1893.

Confederate monument, Greensboro, Georgia.

Confederate monument, to Confederate General Joseph E. Johnston, "one of the greatest generals the world has produced," Dalton, Georgia.

Confederate monument, Hawkinsville, Georgia, 1908.

Confederate monument, unveiling ceremony, LaGrange, Georgia, 1902.

Confederate monument, Court House square, Lumpkin, Georgia, 1908.

Confederate monument, Macon Georgia, 1912.

Confederate monument, Marietta, Georgia, 1908.

Dedication ceremony of the Confederate monument above, at Marietta, Georgia, July 7, 1908.

Confederate monument, to Confederate Captain Matthew Talbot Nunnally, Rest Haven Cemetery, Monroe, Georgia.

Confederate monument, Monticello, Georgia.

Confederate monument, public square, Newnan, Georgia, 1885.

Confederate monument, Myrtle Hill Cemetery, Rome, Georgia, 1887.

Confederate monument, to the women of the Confederacy, Rome, Georgia, 1910. One of the inscriptions on the memorial was written by soon to be U.S. President Woodrow Wilson.

Confederate monument, to Tennessee alderman, sheriff, and Confederate General Nathan Bedford Forrest, Broad St., Rome, Georgia, 1908.

Confederate monument, the Parade Ground, Savannah, Georgia, 1875.

Confederate Memorial Hall, 808 Drayton St., Savannah, Georgia.

Confederate monument, "The Confederate," Forsyth Park, Savannah, Georgia.

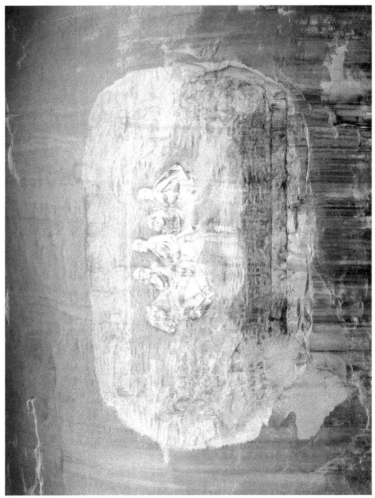

Confederate monument, rock-relief of Confederate icons (left to right): Jefferson Davis, Robert E. Lee, and Stonewall Jackson, Stone Mountain Park, Stone Mountain, Georgia.

Closeup of rock carving at Stone Mountain, Georgia (previous page).

Confederate monument, Thomaston, Georgia, 1908.

Confederate monument, Vienna, Georgia, 1908.

Confederate monument, public square, West Point, Georgia, 1901.

INSCRIPTION ON A CONFEDERATE MONUMENT

Soldiers, you in the wreck of gray
With the brazen belt of the C.S.A.,
Take our love and tears to-day.
Take, then, all that we have to give,
And by God's help while our heart shall live
It shall keep in its faithful way
The camp fire lit for the men in gray—
Aye, till trumpet sound far away
And the silver bugle of heaven play
And the roll is called at the judgment day.

No more they hear the rebel yell,
Where battle thunders rose and fell;
'Tis now a welcome and a cheer
To friends, to foemen, far and near;
And peace, sweet peace, born of despair;
Walks forth and sheds her radiance fair
Upon lost fields of honor.

A 73 year old Confederate veteran
posing with his uniform around 1912.

ILLINOIS

Confederate monument, Alton, Illinois.

Decoration of Confederate graves at Oakwood Cemetery, Chicago, Illinois, circa 1894.

Confederate monument dedication, Confederate Mound, Oak Woods Cemetery, 1035 East 67th St., Chicago, Illinois, 1895. This monument was permitted and encouraged in 1881 by Lincoln's son, Robert Todd Lincoln, then Secretary of War under Liberal U.S. President James A. Garfield. Some 100,000 people attended the dedication (shown here) on May 30, including U.S. President Grover Cleveland and his cabinet.

Another view of the Confederate monument dedication at Chicago, Illinois, 1895.

A more recent view of the Confederate monument, Confederate Mound, Oak Woods Cemetery, Chicago, Illinois.

Confederate monument, Rock Island Confederate Cemetery, Rock Island Arsenal, Rock Island, Illinois.

Confederate monument, Confederate Section, Camp Butler National
Cemetery, Springfield, Illinois.

INSCRIPTION ON A CONFEDERATE MONUMENT

Erected in memory of our Confederate soldiers by the United Daughters of the Confederacy, Marshall Chapter (Texas), No. 412. The love, gratitude, and memory of the people of the South shall gild their fame in one eternal sunshine.

Miss Alice Baxter, President Georgia Division, U.D.C., 1910.

INDIANA

Confederate monument, Woodlawn Cemetery, Terre Haute, Indiana.

Closeup of a panel of Confederate monument on previous page, proving
that by law the U.S. government recognizes Confederate soldiers as U.S.
military veterans. Woodlawn Cemetery, Terre Haute, Indiana.

Confederate veteran Capt. W. G. Hawkins, of Company A, Twenty-fourth South Carolina Infantry.

Medal honoring Sumner Archibald Cunningham, founder and editor of *Confederate Veteran* magazine.

Miss Bettina Ruth Bush, a fervent supporter of Confederate soldiers and the Southern Cause, attended the U.C.V. Reunion in New Orleans, Louisiana, in 1903.

One of the author's favorite Confederate soldiers: Christian mystic, Mason, and Confederate General Albert Pike of Boston, Massachusetts.

Miss Anna Jackson Preston of Charlotte, North Carolina, great-granddaughter of Confederate General Stonewall Jackson.

Miss Laure Beauregard Larendon of Atlanta, Georgia, granddaughter of Confederate General Pierre Gustave Toutant Beauregard.

One of the Confederate soldiers' most fiery defenders, Mildred Rutherford, Historian General, U.D.C.

Sumner Archibald Cunningham, founder and editor of *Confederate Veteran* magazine in 1893.

KENTUCKY

Confederate monument, Bradley Cemetery, Augusta, Kentucky, 1903.

Confederate monument, Bardstown Cemetery, Bardstown, Kentucky, 1906.

Confederate monument, Fairview Cemetery, Bowling Green, Kentucky, 1876.

Confederate monument, Battle Grove Cemetery, Cynthiana, Kentucky, 1869.

Confederate monument, Danville, Kentucky, 1910.

Confederate monument, to Confederate President Jefferson Davis, Fairview, Kentucky, 1924.

The Jefferson Davis Monument at Fairview, Kentucky (see previous page), as it appeared in 1917, midway through construction. Today the massive 351 foot tall memorial is part of the Jefferson Davis Monument State Historic Site, located 10 miles east of Hopkinsville, Kentucky.

Confederate monument, to the Unknown Dead, Hopkinsville, Kentucky. Note: this memorial was the result, in great part, of the time and money of a Yankee, John C. Latham of New York.

Confederate monument, Spring Hill Cemetery, Harrodsburg, Kentucky, 1902.

Confederate monument, Lexington, Kentucky.

Confederate monument, to Confederate General John Hunt Morgan, court-house plaza, Lexington, Kentucky, 1909.

Dedication of the Confederate monument to Confederate General John Hunt Morgan above, Lexington, Kentucky, 1911.

Confederate monument, Louisville, Kentucky.

Confederate monument, to Confederate Colonel Robert A. Smith, near Munfordville, Kentucky.

Confederate monument, to Confederate General Felix Kirk Zollicoffer, near Nancy, Kentucky, 1910.

Confederate monument, Court House square, Owensboro, Kentucky, 1900.

Unveiling ceremony of the Confederate monument above right, at Owensboro, Kentucky, September 21, 1900.

Confederate monument, Owingsville Cemetery, Owingsville, Kentucky, 1907.

Confederate monument, to Confederate General Lloyd Tilghman, Paducah, Kentucky, 1909.

Confederate monument, "to our Confederate dead," Oak Grove Cemetery, Paducah, Kentucky, 1910.

Confederate home monument, Peewee Valley Cemetery, Peewee Valley, Kentucky, 1904.

Confederate monument, Battlefield of Perryville, Perryville, Kentucky. Over 400 Confederate soldiers are buried within the cemetery inclosure.

Confederate monument, Courthouse Square, Princeton, Kentucky, 1912.

Helen's father, Confederate Captain Arthur Henley Keller.

Miss Helen Keller, daughter and granddaughter of Confederate officers (right).

Helen's grandfather, Confederate Colonel Charles William Adams.

Battle of Resaca, Georgia, May 13-16, 1864.

LOUISIANA

Confederate monument, Clinton, Louisiana, 1910.

Confederate monument, to Confederate General Camille Armand Jules Marie Prince de Polignac, Mansfield Battlefield Park, Mansfield, Louisiana, 1925.

Confederate monument, to Confederate General Richard Taylor (son of U.S. President Zachary Taylor), Mansfield Battlefield Park, Mansfield, Louisiana, 1925.

Confederate monument, to Confederate President Jefferson Davis, Jefferson Davis Parkway, New Orleans, Louisiana, 1911. Over 20,000 people attended the dedication on February 22. The "Living Confederate Flag" on the right was composed entirely of school children. Inscription on the monument: "Soldier, Statesman, Patriot: His name is enshrined in the hearts of the people for whom he suffered and his deeds are forever wedded to immortality." Davis will always be held in the highest esteem for leading America's Conservative movement between 1861 and 1865.

Confederate monument, to Confederate officer George Moorman, New Orleans, Louisiana.

Confederate General George Moorman.

Confederate Memorial Hall, New Orleans, Louisiana.

Confederate monument, to Confederate General Pierre G. T. Beauregard, Hollywood Cemetery, New Orleans, Louisiana, 1915.

Confederate monument, to Confederate General Robert E. Lee, Lee Circle, New Orleans, Louisiana.

Confederate monument, to Confederate General Albert Sidney Johnston, New Orleans, Louisiana.

Confederate monument, Shreveport, Louisiana, 1906.

Confederate monument, St. Francisville, Louisiana.

Confederate monument, Tangipahoa, Louisiana, 1905.

A young Southern patriot, 7 year old Virginia Arnold Burt, wearing a Confederate Flag dress, 1910.

A new U.S. national flag, proposed by the South in 1913, combines the beloved symbolic banners of America's two great Confederacies: the C.S.A. and the U.S.A. Though Liberals, most Yankees, and South-loathers in general call the idea "preposterous," other countries have done it. One precedent is Britain's "Union Jack," which combines three national flags: the flag of England, the flag of Scotland, and the flag of Ireland. This suggested new U.S. National Flag would show the fraternity between the South and the North, and "would be most delightfully pleasing to the Southern people" since it would recognize and honor the patriotism of the Confederate soldier—*who fought for the government of the Founding Fathers*. Over 100 years later no movement has yet been made toward fulfilling this commonsense proposition.

Thomas Jonathan Jackson Preston of Charlotte, North Carolina, in 1928, great-grandson of Confederate General Stonewall Jackson.

Confederate General Nathan Bedford Forrest. "Once a hero, always a hero."

Nathan Bedford Forrest III (at around 5 years of age), in 1910, the great-grandson of Confederate General Nathan Bedford Forrest. With military blood in his veins, Forrest III rose to the rank of brigadier general in the U.S. Air Force during World War II. He died when the B-17 bomber he was piloting was shot down over Kiel, Germany, in 1943. Posthumously awarded the Distinguished Flying Cross, he was later buried at Arlington National Cemetery. His father, Nathan Bedford Forrest II, was the 19th commander-in-chief of the Sons of Confederate Veterans.

MARYLAND

Confederate monument, Baltimore, Maryland.

Confederate monument, Baltimore, Maryland.

Confederate monument, to the Confederate women of Maryland, Baltimore, Maryland, 1919.

Confederate monument, "to the courage of the Confederate youth," Easton, Maryland.

Confederate monument, Mount Olivet Cemetery, Frederick, Maryland. Some 300 Confederate soldier are buried here.

Confederate monument, to Ridgely Brown and the Confederate soldiers of Montgomery County, Rockville, Maryland, 1913.

Confederate monument, Silver Spring, Maryland (photo from about 1912).

Confederate monument, the church cemetery, Woodside, Maryland, 1896.

Confederate monument, to "the women of the Confederacy," Loudon Park Cemetery, Baltimore, Maryland.

Confederate graves at Loudon Park Cemetery, Baltimore, Maryland.

JEFFERSON DAVIS

Born of a people proud and free,
Nurtured in lore of sovereignty
Of Statehood's rights—of manhood's right
To rend the meaning, in his sight.
Meant by the Fathers writ in words
Of their day's need—

He came in fearless faith to lead
His people at their call, the seed
Of a new nation to implant,
Where pride of race should make no feint
Of closer ties than nature bids
Mankind to make.

Conscious of right, unbent he bore
Defeat and failure, proudly wore
The smile that met the cruel arts
Of dark misfortune, all the darts
That torturing shame and venomed shaft
Could fling and thrust.

Content that coming years would prove
His stainless honor, quenchless love,
That truth impartial does not fail
To make untruth of no avail,
He left to time, whose scales are true,
Its work to do.

Time's work is done. The world of weight
Has placed him with immortals great.
And to his memory stately stone
To-day is reared that it be shown
His name into eternity
Honored shall be.

Son of the South! Anew we swear
Allegiance to those memories dear,
Which time nor place nor power nor might
Can dim or pale or cower or blight,
And to the world we proudly say:
"All hail this day!"[195]

KATE LANGLEY BOSHER

MISSISSIPPI

Confederate monument, Aberdeen Mississippi.

Davis Family Memorial Windows, Church of the Redeemer (Episcopal), Biloxi, Mississippi. From left, first window: "To Varina Howell Davis, by the U.D.C. (1908)." Second window from left: "To the Four Sons of Jefferson Davis, by Mrs. (Margaret Howell Davis) Hayes (1908)." Third window from left: "To President Jefferson Davis, by his wife (1906)." Fourth window from left: "To Varina Anne 'Winnie' Davis, the 'Daughter of the Confederacy,' by Mrs. Jefferson Davis (1906)."

Confederate monument, public square, Brandon, Mississippi, 1907.

Confederate monument, Russell Square, Brookville, Mississippi, 1912.

Confederate monument, Friendship Cemetery, Columbus, Mississippi, 1873.

Confederate monument, to the Confederate soldiers of Lowndes County, Columbus, Mississippi, 1912.

Confederate monument, Southeast Confederate Cemetery, Columbus, Mississippi.

Confederate dead at Corinth National Cemetery, Corinth, Mississippi.

Confederate monument, to Confederate Colonel William P. Rogers, Corinth, Mississippi, 1912.

Confederate monument, Greenwood, Mississippi, 1913.

Confederate monument, to Confederate General and Mississippi Senator Edward C. Walthall, Holly Springs, Mississippi.

Confederate monument, to "Our Unknown Dead," Holly Springs, Mississippi.

Confederate monument, to Confederate President and American statesman Jefferson Davis, Confederate Park, Jackson, Mississippi, 1891.

Confederate monument, Liberty, Mississippi, 1871. Note: Some believe this is the first Confederate monument built after the War, while there are those who claim that that title goes to Bolivar, Tennessee. Still others hold that the first one went up in Romney, West Virginia, in 1867. In any event, Conservative citizens of Liberty are proud to say that their monument was erected during Reconstruction, at the height of the Liberals' nefarious carpetbag-scallywag regime (1865-1877).

Confederate monument, Livingston, Mississippi, 1908.

Confederate monument, Main St., Okolona, Mississippi, 1905.

Confederate monument, public square, Oxford, Mississippi.

Confederate monument, court-house yard, Raymond, Mississippi, 1908.

Confederate monument, to Confederate General and Mississippi State Senator Stephen Dill Lee, Vicksburg, Mississippi.

Confederate monument, Confederate cemetery, Vicksburg, Mississippi.

Confederate tablet, dedicated to Virginia's Botetourt Artillery, Stevenson's Division, Army of Vicksburg, (former) National Park, Vicksburg, Mississippi.

Confederate monument, West Point, Mississippi, 1907.

i

Before Liberals forced their hate-filled, fake Civil War history into our schoolbooks, entire cities once eagerly, respectfully, and lovingly opened their doors to Confederate veterans. This 1893 photo shows a grand Confederate parade in Houston, Texas, during the Great Reunion of United Confederate Veterans (U.C.V.), forerunners of today's Sons of Confederate Veterans (S.C.V.).

The main entrance to Hollywood Cemetery, Richmond, Virginia, where 16,000 brave and patriotic Confederate soldiers rest in eternal peace.

1906 magazine advertisement.

The youngest Confederate in uniform at the 1911 Confederate Veterans Reunion in Little Rock, Arkansas: 4 year old George Bourk of Texarkana, Texas.

Arkansas Confederate Soldiers' Home, Little Rock, Arkansas, 1908.

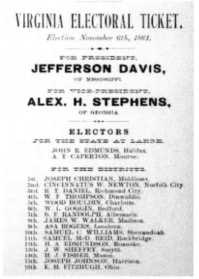

A Virginia electoral ticket, with the election set for November 6, 1861, highlighting Confederate presidential candidate Jefferson Davis, and Confederate vice presidential candidate Alexander H. Stephens.

John Esten Cooke, one of the Confederacy's most beloved poets.

MISSOURI

Confederate monument, Masonic Cemetery, Fredericktown, Missouri.

Confederate monument, Higginsville, Missouri, 1906.

Dedication of the Confederate monument above, at Higginsville, Missouri, 1906.

Confederate monument, Union Cemetery, Kansas City, Missouri.

Confederate monument, Kansas City, Missouri.

Confederate monument, Machpelah Cemetery, Lexington, Missouri, 1896.

Confederate monument, Fairview
Cemetery, Liberty, Missouri, 1904.

Confederate monument, Odd Fellows
Cemetery, Neosho, Missouri, 1902.

Confederate monument, Courthouse Square, Palmyra, Missouri, 1907.

Confederate monument, Confederate Cemetery, Springfield, Missouri, 1901.

Confederate cemetery, Springfield, Missouri, in 1901.

"The Zolnay Confederate Monument," St. Louis, Missouri (photo from around 1912).

After he was released from prison untried and unpunished (for, since secession was legal, no prosecuting attorney could be found to represent the U.S.), Confederate President Jefferson Davis and his wife Varina temporarily resided in Montreal, Canada, at which time this photo was taken.

In 1906, in a postwar demonstration of "good fellowship," Union Capt. Henry S. Cave (left) and Confederate Gen. Andrew J. West (right) posed together at Legget's Hill, where some of the fiercest fighting took place at the Battle of Atlanta, July 22, 1864.

"Southern beauties" supporting the Confederacy at Birmingham, Alabama, circa 1890s.

Four nieces of Confederate boy-hero Sam Davis, 1906. Upper left: Miss Emma C. Davis; Upper right: Miss Media Davis; Lower left: Miss Fannie B. Mathews; Lower right: Mrs. Carrie Tucker Neel.

MONTANA

Confederate Memorial Fountain, Great Northern Park, Last Chance Gulch, Helena, Montana, 1916.

FREEDOM

What right to freedom when we are not free;
When all the passions goad us into lust;
When for the worthless spoil we lick the dust;
And while one-half the people die that we
May sit with peace and freedom 'neath our tree,
The other gloats for plunder and for spoil,
Bustles through daylight, vexes night with toil,
Cheats, swindles, lies, and steals? Shall such things be
Endowed with such grand boons as Liberty
Brings in her train of blessings? Should we pray
That such as these should still maintain the sway—
These soulless, senseless, heartless enemies
Of all that's good and great, of all that's wise,
Worthy on earth or in the Eternal Eyes?[196]

AUTHOR UNKNOWN, 1864

A happy Confederate baby, Hugh T. Morton Jr., 1908.

NEW JERSEY

Confederate monument, Fort Mott (State Park), Pennsville, New Jersey. Some 2,436 Confederate soldiers, who perished at Fort Delaware, are buried here at the National Cemetery on the Delaware River. This monument was erected by the U.S. government under the kind auspices of President William McKinley (served 1897-1901).

Confederate monument, Finn's Point National Cemetery, Salem, New Jersey.

A Chattanooga, Tennessee, organization inviting Confederate men and women to the city, magazine ad, 1913.

Confederate veterans, Warrenton, Virginia, 1903.

A beautiful sight then and now: Louisiana's State Sponsor (center bottom row) and her accompanying Maids of Honor for the U.C.V. Reunion at Louisville, Kentucky, 1900.

The place where Confederate President Jefferson Davis was illegally imprisoned after the War.

Confederate General Edmund Winchester Rucker. The author descends from the Rucker family and is close cousins with the general.

NEW YORK

Confederate section, for the Confederate soldiers who died in Elmira Prison during Lincoln's War, Woodlawn Cemetery, Elmira, New York.

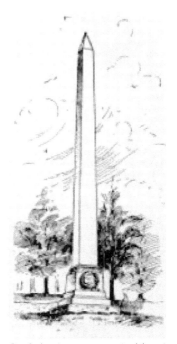

Confederate monument, Mount Hope Cemetery, Hastings-on-Hudson, New York, 1897.

INSCRIPTION ON A CONFEDERATE MONUMENT

They fought for constitutional liberty and State
sovereignty in obedience to the teachings of the Fathers
who framed the Constitution of these United States.

Victorian Southerners taught their children to
honor Confederate soldiers for their patriotism,
fearlessness, valor, military genius, and sacrifices,
and to respect and protect the many Confederate
monuments raised in their memories. Devotion
to Americanism (attachment to the original
Conservative government, principles, practices,
and Constitution created by our Right-wing
Founding Fathers) is alive and well today among
educated modern Southern parents, who—like
their Confederate ancestors—proudly pass these
traditions onto the next generation.

NORTH CAROLINA

Confederate monument, to Confederate Colonel and Governor Zebulon Baird Vance, public square, Asheville, North Carolina, 1898.

Confederate battlefield monument, Averasboro, North Carolina, 1872.

Confederate monument, a Candler cemetery, Candler, North Carolina.

Confederate monument, to nine brothers of the Tolar family, all who perished in Lincoln's War: William J., John H., Robert M., Matthew A., Thomas B., Sampson B., Alfred H., Haynes L., and Joseph M. Cross Creek Cemetery, Fayetteville, North Carolina.

Confederate monument, Cross Creek Cemetery, Fayetteville, North Carolina, 1868.

Confederate monument, St. James Square, Fayetteville, North Carolina, 1902.

Confederate monument, to Jefferson Davis, "Statesmen's Row," in what is known as the South's "Open-Air Westminster," Old Calvary Church, Fletcher, North Carolina, 1931.

Confederate monument, to Orren Randolph Smith, designer of the First National Confederate Flag, the "Stars and Bars," Old Calvary Church, Fletcher, North Carolina, 1930.

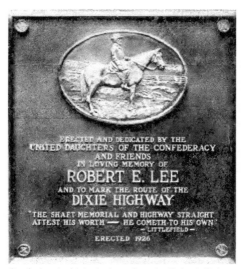

Confederate historical marker, to Robert E. Lee, Dixie Highway, Old Historic Calvary Episcopal Church, Fletcher, North Carolina, 1926.

Confederate monument, to Confederate General and Christian mystic Albert Pike, Old Calvary Church, Fletcher, North Carolina, 1928.

Confederate monument, Franklin, North Carolina, 1909.

Confederate monument, Henderson, North Carolina, 1910.

Confederate monument, Louisburg, North Carolina, 1914.

Confederate Memorial Fountain, Louisburg, North Carolina, 1923. Beneath the Confederate First National Flag carved in the stone is a bronze tablet on which is inscribed: "Erected September, 1923, by the North Carolina Division, United Daughters of the Confederacy, in appreciation of the fact that the first flag of the Confederacy, 'The Stars and Bars,' was designed by a son of North Carolina, Orren Randolph Smith, and made under his direction by Catherine Rebecca (Murphy) Winborne, forwarded to Montgomery, Ala., February 12, 1861, adopted by the Provisional Confederate Congress March 4, 1861. First displayed in North Carolina at Louisburg, March 18, 1861."

Confederate monument, Oxford, North Carolina.

Another view of Confederate monument above, Oxford, North Carolina.

Confederate monument, Pittsboro, North Carolina, 1907.

Confederate monument, Raleigh, North Carolina, 1895.

Confederate monument, to Confederate soldier Henry L. Wyatt, Raleigh, North Carolina, 1912. Wyatt, "who fell at Bethel," was known as "the first Confederate soldier to give up his life for the Southern Cause": Conservatism, also known as Americanism. Thousands attended the dedication on June 9, including people from other cities, as well as Democrat (Liberal) North Carolina Governor William Walton Kitchin.

Confederate monument, Raleigh, North Carolina
(photo from around 1912).

Confederate monument, Roxboro, North Carolina.

Confederate monument, public square, Waynesboro, North Carolina, 1892.

Confederate monument, Wilmington, North Carolina.

Confederate monument, Windsor, North Carolina, 1895.

Confederate monument, Winston, North Carolina.

Confederate monument, town square, Yanceyville, North Carolina.

THE SOUTH

The South is a land that has known sorrow; it is a land that has broken the ashen crust and moistened it with her tears; a land scarred and riven by the plowshare of war and billowed with the graves of her dead; but a land of legend, a land of song, a land of hallowed and heroic memories.

To that land every drop of my blood, every fiber of my being, every pulsation of my heart is consecrated forever. I was born of her womb, I was nourished at her breast, and, when my last hour shall come, I pray God that I may be pillowed upon her bosom and rocked to sleep within her tender and encircling arms.[197]

EDWARD W. CARMACK, TENNESSEE

Battle of Kennesaw Mountain, near Marietta, Georgia, June 24, 1864.

OHIO

Confederate cemetery, Columbus, Ohio. The land and stone wall enclosure that sit upon this "Rebel graveyard" were paid for by the U.S. government.

Confederate memorial stone, to Confederate General John Hunt Morgan, East Liverpool, Ohio, 1909.

Confederate memorial, to Daniel Decatur Emmett, composer of the song "Dixie," Emmett's grave site, Mound View Cemetery, Mount Vernon, Ohio, 1915.

Confederate memorial, to Daniel Decatur Emmett, composer of the song "Dixie," Mount Vernon, Ohio, 1931.

Confederate monument, "The Lookout," Confederate Stockade Cemetery, Johnson's Island, Sandusky, Ohio.

Confederate veteran Reverend James M. Mason of the 4th Alabama Cavalry.

This 1914 ad for Virginia's Stonewall Jackson College for Girls and Young Women (named by General Robert E. Lee), illustrates how widely accepted the Confederacy and her heroes were before the history of Lincoln's War was intentionally and treacherously rewritten by South-hating Liberals, socialists, and communists.

OKLAHOMA

Confederate monument, Fairlawn Cemetery, Oklahoma City, Oklahoma, 1923.

INSCRIPTION ON A CONFEDERATE MONUMENT

In honor of
The heroes who fell
While fighting for us
In the Army of
The Confederate States,
1861-1865.

Though adverse fortune
Denied final victory
To their undaunted courage,
History preserves their fame,
Made glorious forever.

Miss Alleen Smith, Confederate Maid of
Honor, Forrest's Cavalry, 1911.

PENNSYLVANIA

Confederate battlefield monument, to Maryland's 2nd Infantry, C.S.A., Culp's Hill, Gettysburg, Pennsylvania, 1886.

Confederate Cavalry Avenue, Gettysburg National Military Park, Gettysburg, Pennsylvania.

Confederate monument, to the Confederate soldiers of North Carolina, Gettysburg National Military Park, Gettysburg, Pennsylvania, 1929.

Another view of the monument to the Confederate soldiers of North Carolina (above), Gettysburg National Military Park, Gettysburg, Pennsylvania.

Confederate monument, from Virginia to her Confederate sons at the Battle of Gettysburg, Gettysburg, Pennsylvania, 1917.

Confederate monument, Pittville National Cemetery, Philadelphia, Pennsylvania, circa 1911. Erected by the U.S. government in honor of the 184 Confederate soldiers and sailors who died while held in Yankee prisons in the cities of Chester, Pennsylvania, and Philadelphia, Pennsylvania.

INSCRIPTION ON A CONFEDERATE MONUMENT

They gave their all in defense of home, honor, liberty, and the independence of their native land. They fought the valorous fight. They kept the faith of their fathers, forever honored and forever mourned.

A 1916 magazine ad for the McNeel Marble Company of Marietta, Georgia.

SOUTH CAROLINA

Confederate monument, Aiken, South Carolina, 1901.

Confederate monument, a plaza on the square, Anderson, South Carolina, 1901.

Confederate monument, Magnolia Cemetery, Charleston, South Carolina, 1882.

Closeup of the Confederate monument
above, Magnolia Cemetery, Charleston,
South Carolina.

Confederate monument, to the Washington Light Infantry, Washington Park, Charleston, South Carolina, 1891. Named after George Washington, the WLI was founded in 1807, and later, as a Confederate command, fought for the South in numerous battles during Lincoln's War. It is exists to this day and is considered one of America's oldest military units.

Confederate monument, Chester, South Carolina, 1905.

Confederate monument, Clinton, South Carolina, 1911.

Confederate monument, cemetery of the St. David Episcopal Church, Cheraw, South Carolina, unveiled June 1867. Like many others, this monument is claimed by its originators, the Cheraw Ladies' Memorial Association, to be the first one ever raised to the Confederate dead.

Confederate General Maxcy Gregg.

Confederate monument, to Confederate General Maxcy Gregg, Columbia, South Carolina.

Confederate monument, Columbia, South Carolina, 1879.

Confederate monument, to Confederate General, Governor, and Senator Wade Hampton, State House grounds, Columbia, South Carolina, 1906.

Confederate monument, to the Confederate women of South Carolina, Columbia, South Carolina, 1912.

Confederate monument, Edgefield, South
Carolina, 1908.

Confederate monument, Fort Mill, South
Carolina, 1891.

INSCRIPTION ON THE
WOMEN'S MONUMENT (left)

Affectionately dedicated by the
Jefferson Davis Memorial Association
to the Women of the Confederacy, the
living and the dead, who midst the
gloom of war were heroines in the
strife to perpetuate their noble
sacrifices on the altar of our common
country. Let sweet incense forever
rise, till it reach them in robes of
victory beyond the skies.

Confederate monument, to the
Women of the Confederacy, Fort Mill,
South Carolina, 1895.

INSCRIPTION ON THE
SLAVES' MONUMENT (right)

Dedicated to the faithful slaves
who, loyal to a sacred trust, toiled
for the support of the Army with
matchless devotion, and with
sterling fidelity guarded our
defenseless homes, women, and
children during the struggle for the
principles of our Confederate States
of America. Erected . . . with the
approval of the Jefferson Davis
Memorial Association.

Confederate monument, to "Faithful
Slaves," Fort Mill, South Carolina, 1891.

Confederate monument, Georgetown, South Carolina.

Confederate monument, Greenville, South Carolina.

Confederate monument, a public square, Jonesville, South Carolina, 1907.

Confederate monument, Lancaster, South Carolina, 1909.

Confederate monument, to Calvin Crozier, Rosemont Cemetery, Newberry, South Carolina, 1891.

Confederate monument, Newberry, South Carolina, 1893.

Confederate Memorial Drinking Fountain, St. Matthews, South Carolina, 1924.

CONFEDERATE MAJOR ROBERT STILES' TRIBUTE TO ROBERT E. LEE

There could never have been a second "Marse Robert"; as, but for the unparalleled elevation and majesty of his character and bearing, there would never have been the first. He was of all men most attractive to us, yet by no means most approachable. We loved him much, but we revered him more. We never criticised, never doubted him, never attributed to him either moral error or mental weakness—no, not even in our secret hearts or most audacious thoughts. I really believe it would have strained and blurred our strongest and clearest conceptions of the distinction between right and wrong to have entertained even for a moment the thought that he had ever acted from any other than the purest and loftiest motive. I never but once heard of such a suggestion, and then it so transported the hearers that military subordination was forgotten, and the colonel who heard it rushed with drawn sword against the major-general who made it.[198]

Magazine ad for a Yankee metalworks, the American Bronze Foundry Company, soliciting Confederate business in 1910.

TENNESSEE

Confederate monument, court house square, Bolivar, Tennessee.

Confederate monument, Brownsville, Tennessee, 1908.

Confederate monument, memorializing the birthplace of Confederate General Nathan Bedford Forrest, Chapel Hill, Tennessee. Note: The original house no longer stands. (Photo Lochlainn Seabrook)

Confederate monument, to Carnes' Battery, National Cemetery, Chattanooga, Tennessee, raised 1898.

Confederate monument, to Tennessee's Confederate soldiers, Chickamauga Military Park, near Chattanooga, Tennessee.

Confederate monument, Clarksville, Tennessee, 1893.

Confederate monument, Confederate section, to "Our Fallen Heroes," Rose Hill Cemetery, Columbia, Tennessee. (Photo Lochlainn Seabrook)

Confederate monument, to the Battle of Britton's Lane, near Denmark, Tennessee, 1898.

Confederate monument, court house yard, Dyersburg, Tennessee, 1905.

Dedication of the Confederate monument, Dyersburg, Tennessee, April 6, 1905, on the anniversary of the Battle of Shiloh.

Confederate monument, Erwin, Tennessee, early 1900s. Note the complete acceptance of combining U.S. symbols and Confederate symbols.

Confederate memorial drinking fountain, to the women of the Confederacy, Confederate Park, Fayetteville, Tennessee, 1914.

Confederate monument, Fayetteville, Tennessee. (Photo Lochlainn Seabrook)

Another view, 100 years older, of Confederate monument at bottom left of previous page, Fayetteville, Tennessee, 1906.

Confederate monument, Franklin, Tennessee, 1899. Notes: the Confederate soldier on top is nicknamed "Chip" due to a piece missing from the brim of his hat; see Appendix B. (Photo Lochlainn Seabrook)

Confederate monument, dedicated to Freeman's Battery, Forrest's Artillery, Winstead Hill, Franklin, Tennessee. (Photo Lochlainn Seabrook)

Confederate memorial, site near the original Carter (family) Gin House, central theater of action during the Battle of Franklin II, Franklin, Tennessee. (Photo Lochlainn Seabrook)

McGavock Confederate Cemetery, with Confederate Carnton Plantation in the background, Franklin, Tennessee. Note: See Appendix C. (Photo Lochlainn Seabrook)

The Trousdale Confederate Home and Monument, Gallatin, Tennessee.

Confederate monument, Lebanon, Tennessee, 1899.

Confederate monument, to Confederate General Robert Hopkins Hatton and the
Confederate soldiers of Wilson County, Lebanon, Tennessee. 1912.

Confederate monument, Lewisburg, Tennessee, 1907.

Confederate monument, to Confederate Captain J. Harvey Mathes, Elmwood Cemetery, Memphis, Tennessee, 1907.

Confederate monument, to Memphis alderman and Confederate General Nathan Bedford Forrest, Memphis, Tennessee, 1905.

INSCRIPTION

Erected by his countrymen in honor
Of the military genius of
Lieutenant-General Nathan Bedford Forrest.
Confederate States Army.
1861-1865.

Those hoof beats die not upon fame's crimsoned sod,
But will ring through her song and her story;
He fought like a titan and struck like a god,
And his dust is our ashes of glory.

Confederate monument, Mount Pleasant, Tennessee, 1907.
(Photo Lochlainn Seabrook)

Confederate monument, Mulberry, Tennessee, 1909.

Confederate monument, Battle of Murfreesboro battlefield, Murfreesboro, Tennessee. Erected by the Nashville, Chattanooga, and St. Louis Railway Company.

Confederate monument, to the "Private Soldiers," Centennial Park, Nashville, Tennessee, 1909. (Photo Lochlainn Seabrook)

Dedication of the Confederate monument to the "Private Soldiers" at the bottom of previous page, Centennial Park, Nashville, Tennessee, 1909.

Confederate monument, to the innocent and brave 21 year old Sam Davis, Confederate soldier and martyr to the Southern Cause, Nashville, Tennessee, 1909.

INSCRIPTION

Though a Confederate soldier in the line of duty, he was executed as a spy by the Federals at Pulaski, Nov. 27, 1863.

This monument is erected by contributions from citizens Of every state in the American union. On the site authorized by the 51ˢᵗ General Assembly Of the state of Tennessee.

Dedication of the Confederate monument to Sam Davis, Nashville, Tennessee, April 29, 1909. Thousands attended and the main address was presented by Tennessee Governor Malcolm Rice Patterson.

Elizabeth Davis, grandniece of Sam Davis, who unveiled his monument in Nashville in 1909.

Confederate monument, Confederate Circle, Mount Olivet Cemetery, Nashville, Tennessee. (Photo Lochlainn Seabrook)

Confederate monument, Paris, Tennessee, 1900. Note: See Appendix D.

Confederate monument, to Confederate hero-martyr Sam Davis, Pulaski, Tennessee. (Photo Lochlainn Seabrook)

Confederate fountain, honoring the Confederate soldiers of Lauderdale County, Ripley, Tennessee.

Confederate monument, featuring a cannon from Ft. Pillow, Ripley, Tennessee.

Confederate monument, to Sumner Archibald Cunningham, a Confederate veteran and the founder (and editor) of *Confederate Veteran* magazine in 1893, Willow Mount Cemetery, Shelbyville, Tennessee, 1921.

Confederate monument, dedication, October 17, 1899, Confederate Square, Willow Mount Cemetery, Shelbyville, Tennessee. Some 600 Confederate soldiers are buried here.

Dedication of the Confederate monument, Shiloh, Tennessee.

Confederate monument, to Alabama's Confederate troops, Shiloh National Military Park, Shiloh, Tennessee, 1907.

Confederate monument, to the Confederate Arkansas troops who perished at the Battle of Shiloh, Shiloh National Military Park, Shiloh, Tennessee, 1910.

Confederate monument, to Confederate General Albert Sidney Johnston, Shiloh National Military Park, Shiloh, Tennessee. Erected by the U.S. government.

Confederate monument, Shiloh National Military Park, Shiloh, Tennessee.

Confederate monument, to Louisiana's Confederate troops at the Battle of Shiloh, Shiloh, Tennessee.

Confederate monument, to the Confederate martyr-hero, young Sam Davis, Smyrna, Tennessee. (Erected by his father Charles.)

Confederate monument, to Forrest's first artillery captain, Samuel L. Freeman, who though unarmed and surrendered at the time, was cruelly and wantonly killed by his Yankee captors, Spring Hill Cemetery, Spring Hill, Tennessee. Note: there is a small Confederate section in this public cemetery, where rest the bodies of some of the South's best men. (Photo Lochlainn Seabrook)

Text on reverse side of Confederate monument above left, describing Capt. Freeman's military service and murder, Spring Hill Cemetery, Spring Hill, Tennessee. (Photo Lochlainn Seabrook)

Confederate monument, to the Kentuckians (under Forrest) who perished at the Battle of Tarpley, September 27, 1864, Tarpley Shop, Tennessee, 1912.

Confederate monument, to Roderick, famed warhorse of Confederate General Nathan Bedford Forrest, killed at the Battle of Thompson's Station, March 5, 1863, Thompson's Station, Tennessee. (Photo Lochlainn Seabrook)

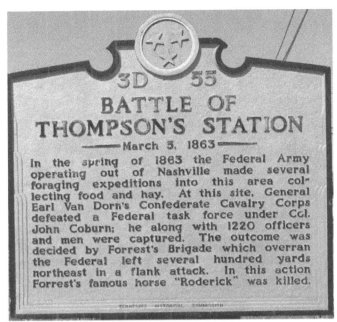

Historical marker describing the Battle of Thompson's Station and the loss of Roderick, Thompson's Station, Tennessee. (Photo Lochlainn Seabrook)

Confederate monument, Trenton, Tennessee.

Confederate monument, Union City, Tennessee, 1912.

TO THE CONFEDERATE DEAD

Thousands of brave men had given their lives for that which in the eyes of the world was utter failure with the stamp of treason upon it. Their government had vanished; their record was in the hands of their late foes. The history writers called their action rebellion and insurrection. The [U.S.] government to which they had submitted, in its public acts and laws, did the same. They had done all that men could do, and when all further effort was impossible they had submitted with dignity and in good faith.

But that good faith did not imply a forgetfulness by the living of duty to the dead. Those dead heroes had no government to protect their memories or to honor their graves. They died battling for us, and some perpetual mark of our appreciation is due, not merely as an honor to their memory, but to stand as a living witness in future years that they were not regarded as traitors by their own people, and that we delight to do them honor.[199]

ALBERT T. McNEAL

Truce at the Battle of Kennesaw Mountain, June 27, 1864, proposed by Confederate soldiers when they saw that some Union soldiers had been burned by forest fire. "They helped to save their enemies."

TEXAS

Confederate monument, Amarillo, Texas.

Confederate monument, to Confederate
General John Bell Hood's Texas Brigade,
capitol grounds, Austin, Texas, 1910.

Confederate monument, to Terry's Texas Rangers, capitol grounds, Austin, Texas, 1907.

Confederate monument, to Confederate General Thomas "Tom" Green, Oakwood Cemetery, Austin, Texas, 1909.

Confederate monument, Bonham, Texas.

Confederate memorial, to Jefferson Davis, Jefferson Davis Highway,
Brownsville, Texas, 1927.

Confederate monument, Corsicana, Texas, 1908.

Confederate monument, to Robert E. Lee and his warhorse Traveller, Oak Lawn, Dallas, Texas.

Confederate monument, the "Grand Monument," to "Our Sacred Cause," Dallas, Texas, 1897.

Dedication of the Grand Monument above, Dallas, Texas, April 29, 1897.

Confederate monument, City Park, Gainesville, Texas, 1908. Note: See Appendix E.

"The Confederate Soldiers and Sailors Monument," Williamson County court house square, Georgetown, Texas, 1916.

Confederate monument, Gonzales, Texas, 1910.

Confederate monument, to Confederate Major Richard W. "Dick" Dowling, City Hall, Houston, Texas.

Confederate monument, Monument Park (town center), Jefferson, Texas, 1907.

Confederate monument, County Courthouse yard, Linden, Texas, 1903.

Confederate monument, court house yard, Marshall, Texas, 1906.

Confederate monument, to Confederate Secretary of the Treasury and Texas Senator John Henninger Reagan, Palestine, Texas.

Confederate monument, "The Lost Cause,"
Palestine, Texas.

Confederate monument, Paris, Texas, 1903.

Confederate monument, Court House square, Rusk, Texas, 1907.

Confederate monument, to the Confederate soldiers who fought at the Battle of Sabine Pass, Sabine Pass, Port Arthur, Texas, 1924.

Confederate monument, Travis Park, San Antonio, Texas, 1900.

Confederate monument, Sherman, Texas.

Confederate monument, "The Last Stand," Victoria, Texas, 1912.

Dedication of the Confederate monument above, July 10, 1912, Victoria, Texas. Around 2,000 people attended.

Confederate monument, Ellis County Courthouse, Waxahachie, Texas.

INSCRIPTION ON A CONFEDERATE MONUMENT

This Carven Stone is Here to Tell
To All the World the Love We Bear
To Those Who Fought and Bled and Fell,
Whose Battle Cry was Do and Dare.
Who Feared No Foe, but Faced the Fray—
Our Gallant Men Who Wore the Gray.

Confederate General Patrick R. Cleburne's Division repulsing Sherman's forces at the
Battle of Missionary Ridge, November 25, 1863.

DESCRIPTION OF A TYPICAL CONFEDERATE VETERAN

He is tall, strong, and erect, gray-haired, fiery-eyed, soft voiced, and gentle of manner. He fought through the four years' war with the energy, dash, and courage for which he was famous, and at the end—when the South surrendered—faced that situation with as much heroism as he had displayed in battle. After nearly forty years of the new regime, our veteran considers himself "reconstructed," although he always votes with the "Solid South." On the whole he accepts the situation philosophically, and he gave his only son Godspeed when he answered his country's call for the Spanish-American war [1898] and marched away in the uniform of blue.

We who love our veteran best know, however, that behind the closed door of his heart the ruined cause is deeply, tenderly, solemnly enshrined, and will be for aye. We regard the sentiment with reverence and silence, as when you walk softly in the presence of sacred dead. Though so fiery-tempered and quick-spoken, like the men of his kind and vicinity, he is very gentle and tender to the young; so he is at his best when in the society of the little ones, who have for him that "perfect love which casteth out fear."

The grandchildren of a man of this type were dressed for a Decoration Day celebration to be given at school some time since. They wore white, gayly adorned in ribbons of red-white and-blue. Each little girl had a plant to carry, and they were full of excitement and joy at the prospect of the celebration before them. "O grandpa," said the youngest child, "we are going to have a splendid entertainment at school to-day. We are going to sing 'America,' 'The Star-Spangled Banner,' 'Tenting To-Night,' and 'Rally Round the Flag, Boys.' We are taking flowers for the soldiers' graves, and we are going to salute the flag, grandpa, this way." And she saluted.

He was looking with interest and love at his darling, enjoying her pleasure and excitement, when his expression changed and softened, his clear face quivered just an instant, and he spoke very softly and gently: "Sing them all, my baby; take your flowers and salute your flag, but when you have finished it all ask your teacher to let you sing 'Dixie' and the 'Days of Auld Lang Syne,' for grandpa."[200] — Year, 1903

VIRGINIA

Confederate monument, Court House square,
Abingdon, Virginia, 1907.

Road marker denoting the Jefferson Davis
Highway in Virginia.

Confederate monument, Alexandria, Virginia (photo from around 1919).

Confederate plaque, marking the spot where Confederate General Robert E. Lee waited for a flag of truce from Union General Ulysses S. Grant, Appomattox Court House, Virginia.

Confederate monument, courthouse yard, Appomattox, Virginia, 1906.

Confederate Monument, Arlington National Cemetery, Arlington, Virginia (photo from around 1921). This beautiful monument was petitioned by the United Daughters of the Confederacy, which was granted by then Secretary of War William Howard Taft on March 4, 1906. The designer chosen was acclaimed sculptor and Confederate veteran Moses Ezekiel. Eventually 482 individuals were buried in the Confederate section surrounding the monument, including not only 46 Confederate officers and 351 soldiers, but 58 Southern women, 15 civilians, and 12 unknowns.

Another view of the Confederate Monument, Arlington National Cemetery, Arlington, Virginia (photo from around 1915).

U.S. President Warren G. Harding speaking at the dedication services for the Confederate Monument, Arlington National Cemetery, Arlington, Virginia, June 4-5 1922.

Arlington House, former residence of Confederate General Robert E. Lee, Arlington National Cemetery, Arlington, Virginia, photo taken June 29, 1864. Now owned by the U.S. government, it is America's premier memorial to the South's most famous military officer. (Note U.S. soldiers posing near the front portico.)

Confederate monument, to the Confederate soldiers and sailors of Bedford County, Bedford City, Virginia, 1909.   Note: Union veterans contributed funds to help build and raise this memorial.

Confederate monument, Courthouse Square, Boydton, Virginia.

Confederate monument, Buckingham, Virginia, 1908.

Confederate monument, to the Botetourt Artillery, Buchanan, Virginia.

Confederate monument, Charlottesville, Virginia, 1893.

Confederate monument, Charlottesville, Virginia, circa 1909.

Confederate monument, court green, town center, Chatham, Virginia, 1899.

Confederate monument, courthouse green, Covington, Virginia, 1911.

Confederate monument, Fairfax, Virginia, 1904.

Confederate monument, Farmville, Virginia, 1900.

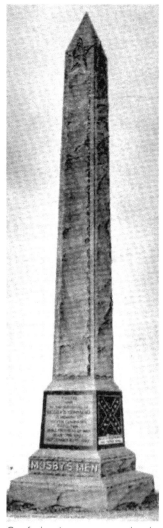

Confederate monument, to Confederate Colonel John Singleton Mosby's men, Front Royal, Virginia, 1899.

Confederate monument, to "our heroes in gray," Hanover Court House, Virginia, 1914.

Confederate monument, to Joseph White Latimer, "the boy major of the Confederacy," Woodbine Cemetery, Harrisonburg, Virginia, 1914.

Confederate monument, to Confederate General Turner Ashby, on a hill two miles southeast of town, Harrisonburg, Virginia, 1897.

Confederate monument, Woodbine Cemetery, Harrisonburg, Virginia, 1876.

Confederate monument, Carroll County Courthouse, Hillsville, Virginia.

Confederate monument, King George, Virginia (photo taken 1921).

Confederate monument, court house lawn, Leesburg, Virginia, 1908.

Lee Chapel, Washington and Lee University, Lexington, Virginia.

Interior of Lee Chapel, Washington and Lee University, Lexington, Virginia, with General Robert E. Lee's recumbent statue just visible at the far end.

Closeup of Confederate General Robert E. Lee's recumbent statue, Lee Chapel, Washington and Lee University, Lexington, Virginia.

Confederate monument, to Confederate General Stonewall Jackson,
Presbyterian Church Cemetery, Lexington, Virginia, 1891.

Confederate monument, "Virginia Mourning Her Dead," in honor of the cadets of the Virginia Military Institute who fought at the Battle of New Market, Memorial Hall, Virginia Military Institute, Lexington, Virginia, 1903.

Confederate monument, Luray, Virginia, 1899.

Confederate monument, soldiers' cemetery, Lynchburg, Virginia.

Confederate monument, Lynchburg, Virginia, 1899.

Confederate monument, court house square, Martinsville, Virginia, 1901.

Confederate monument, to Confederate Captain Sally Louisa Tompkins, Christ Church Cemetery, Mathews, Virginia, 1925.

Confederate monument, Mathews Courthouse, Virginia, 1912.

Confederate monument, Confederate Cemetery, Mount Jackson, Virginia, 1903.

Confederate monument, to the Confederate Dead, Mount Vernon, Virginia.

Confederate monument, St. Matthew's Cemetery, New Market, Virginia, 1898.

Confederate monument, to Confederate Capt. George W. Summers and Confederate Sgt. I. Newton Koontz, three miles north of New Market, Virginia. The innocent pair were cruelly executed (without trial) after the War by Union troops under the command of Yank Lieut. Col . Cyrus Hussy of Ohio.

Confederate monument, Pleasant Grove Baptist Church, Pleasant Grove (District), Norfolk County, Virginia, 1905.

Confederate monument, Commercial Square, Norfolk, Virginia.

Another view of the Confederate monument above, Norfolk, Virginia.

Confederate monument, Parksley, Virginia, 1896.

Confederate battlefield monument, Battle of the Crater site, Petersburg, Virginia, 1924.

A rare "peace monument" dedicated to both U.S. and C.S. troops, Portsmouth, Virginia, 1906. The monument commemorates those Virginians who served with the Portsmouth Light Artillery, which existed from 1809 to 1862: antebellum U.S. soldiers fought with the PLA at the Battle of Craney Island, June 22, 1813; Confederate soldiers fought with the PLA for the first two years of Lincoln's War in such conflicts as Malvern Hill, Second Manassas, and Sharpsburg, the last at which their commander, Capt. Carey F. Grimes, was killed. Though it was then disbanded, the command was reorganized after the War.

Confederate monument, Portsmouth, Virginia.

Confederate monument, public square, town court house, Princess Anne, Virginia, 1905.

The Confederate Memorial Institute, or Battle Abbey, Richmond, Virginia.

Confederate monument, to Mexican War hero, U.S. Secretary of War, Mississippi Senator, and Confederate President Jefferson Davis, Richmond, Virginia, 1907.

Thousands turn out for the dedication of the Jefferson Davis monument above, Richmond, Virginia. Note: See Appendix F.

Design drawing of a stained glass window commemorating Confederate Captain Sally Louisa Tompkins, St. James Episcopal Church, Richmond, Virginia.

Stained glass memorial window, dedicated to Confederate hero-martyr Sam Davis, Tennessee Room, Confederate Museum, Richmond, Virginia, 1912.

A "living Confederate Battle Flag" in front of the Robert E. Lee monument, Confederate Veterans Reunion, Richmond, Virginia, 1910.

Confederate monument, to Confederate General Ambrose Powell Hill, near Richmond, Virginia.

Confederate monument, to Confederate General Robert E. Lee, Richmond, Virginia, 1890.

Another view of the Confederate monument to Confederate General Robert E. Lee, Richmond, Virginia.

Confederate monument, to U.S. President—and later a member of both the Confederate Provisional Congress and member-elect of the permanent Confederate Congress—John Tyler, Hollywood Cemetery, Richmond, Virginia, set up by the U.S. government in 1915. *Confederate Veteran* writes: "And now the Federal government has erected this monument over President Tyler's mortal body; but the significance of the act does not lie in the cost nor in the beauty of the memorial itself. Its erection is unique in that it is the first monument to be voted by the Federal Congress to any man whose sense of duty impelled him to take sides with the South in the stormy days of secession. Viewed in this light, this memorial shaft to John Tyler is the most impressive and significant of all memorial structures in the United States; for it is the first in which both North and South have freely joined, and it stands to the world as the sign and pledge of a reunited country and a testimony that the passions of the past have perished."

Confederate monument, to Confederate General Jeb Stuart, Richmond, Virginia, 1907.

Confederate monument, Hollywood Cemetery, site of the graves of 16,000 Confederate soldiers, Richmond, Virginia, 1869.

Another view of the previous Confederate monument, Hollywood Cemetery, Richmond, Virginia.

Confederate monument, to the soldiers and sailors of the Confederate army and navy, Libby Hill Park, Richmond, Virginia.

Confederate monument, to Varina Anne "Winnie" Davis, Hollywood Cemetery, Richmond, Virginia.

Another view of the Confederate monument to the soldiers and sailors of the Confederate army and navy (previous page), Libby Hill Park, Richmond, Virginia.

Confederate monument, to Confederate official Matthew Fontaine Maury, Richmond, Virginia, 1928.

Confederate monument, to the "Unknown Confederate Dead," Fisher's Hill, near Strasburg, Virginia.

Confederate monument ("The Tom Smith Monument"), Cedar Hill Cemetery, Suffolk, Virginia, 1889.

Confederate monument, Surry, Virginia, 1910.

Confederate monument, Tappahannock, Virginia.

Confederate monument, courthouse, Winchester, Virginia, 1916. During the unveiling ceremony the song "Dixie" was played. The event was well attended, with not only Confederate veterans and U.S. government officials, but students from the High School, Fort Loudon Seminary, and a corps of cadets from the Shenandoah Valley Academy.

Confederate monument, Woodstock, Virginia, 1899.

Confederate monument, Wytheville, Virginia, 1900.

Another view of the Confederate monument to Confederate General Robert E. Lee, Richmond, Virginia, 1890.

GENERAL ORDER NO. 9

After four years of arduous service, marked by unsurpassed courage and fortitude, the Army of Northern Virginia has been compelled to yield to overwhelming numbers and resources.

I need not tell the brave survivors of so many hard-fought battles, who have remained steadfast to the last, that I have consented to this result from no distrust of them. But feeling that valor and devotion could accomplish nothing that would compensate for the loss that must have attended the continuation of the contest, I determined to avoid the sacrifice of those whose past services have endeared them to their countrymen.

By the terms of agreement officers and men can return to their homes and remain until exchanged.

You will take with you the satisfaction that proceeds from the consciousness of duty faithfully performed, and I earnestly pray that a merciful God will extend to you his blessing and protection.

With an unceasing admiration of your constancy and devotion to your country and a grateful remembrance of your kind and generous consideration of myself, I bid you an affectionate farewell.

HEADQUARTERS A.N.V., APRIL 10, 1865
GENERAL ROBERT E. LEE

Confederate veterans, Chattanooga, Tennessee, 1913.

Confederate General Stand Watie, one of the 70,000 Native-Americans who fought under the Confederate Flag.

Robert E. Lee IV, circa 1928. From the original caption: "The 'Little General,' who unveiled the statue of his great-grandfather at Stone Mountain, Georgia, is shown here in the Confederate uniform which he wears as a member of the staff of Mayor [James John 'Jimmy'] Walker, of New York City. He is a manly little fellow of five years."

U.D.C. members unveiling the floral design at the base of the Confederate Monument at Arlington National Cemetery.

Confederate girl, Marietta Randolph Bridger.

"O'er those who lost and those who won,
Death holds no parley which was right—
Jehovah judges."

WASHINGTON, D.C.

Monument of Confederate President Jefferson Davis, on the commemoration of his 130th birthday, June 4, 1938; placing the wreath is Miss Imogene Smith, President of the Charles M. Stedman Children of the Confederacy; to her right is Mrs. Walter D. Lamar, National President of the United Daughters of the Confederacy; on the left is Senator Walter F. George, of Georgia. Location: National Statuary Hall, U.S. Capitol Building, Washington, D.C. Note: See Appendix G. (Notice statue of General Robert E. Lee on the right.)

Monument of Confederate General Robert E. Lee, National Statuary Hall, U.S. Capitol Building, Washington, D.C.

Confederate monument, to Confederate Colonel and Governor Zebulon Baird Vance, National Statuary Hall, U.S. Capitol Building, Washington, D.C.

Victorian Southern men rightly considered Victorian Southern women the backbone of the Confederacy. This group of strong Conservative Confederate women is from Shiloh, Tennessee, circa 1912.

The tallest Confederate soldier: Col. H. C. Thruston of Texas, stood 7 feet 7 inches tall.

Proud Confederate veterans gather for a reunion at Altus, Oklahoma, circa 1912.

Wartime residence of Confederate Vice President Alexander H. Stephens, Richmond, Virginia.

Jefferson Davis' former residence Beauvoir, serving as the Mississippi Confederate Soldiers' Home at the time of this photo, early 1900s.

Inauguration of Confederate President Jefferson Davis, Montgomery, Alabama, 1861.

WEST VIRGINIA

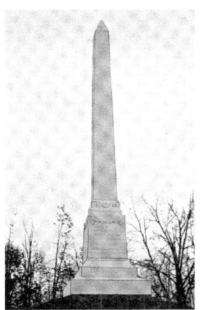

Confederate monument, Mount Iser Cemetery, Beverly, West Virginia, 1908.

Confederate monument, to Confederate General Stonewall Jackson, Charleston, West Virginia, 1910.

Confederate monument, to Confederate General Stonewall Jackson, Harrison County Courthouse, Clarksburg, Virginia.

Confederate monument, Huntington, West Virginia, 1900.

Confederate monument, City Park, Parkersburg, West Virginia, 1908.

Entrance sign to one of America's many cemeteries that contain either Confederate graves or Confederate monuments or both. This one is in Romney, West Virginia.

Confederate monument, Romney, West Virginia (formerly in Virginia), raised in the summer of 1867 and dedicated that year on September 28. Note: despite other claims to the contrary, this is probably the earliest and thus the first Confederate monument to have been erected in the U.S.

Confederate monument and Confederate cemetery,
Shepherdstown, West Virginia, 1869-1870.

Confederate monument, Union, West Virginia, 1901.

Confederate monument (on a high hill on Dr. Cameron's land near the highest gap in Valley Mountain), Valley Mountain, West Virginia, 1902.

The End

Confederate veterans, both white and black, gather at Huntsville, Alabama, in 1928.

"LOVE MAKES MEMORY ETERNAL." —— U.D.C. MOTTO, 1915

Confederate veterans, Company B, Regular Tennessee Militia, Nashville, 1902.

INSCRIPTION ON A CONFEDERATE MONUMENT

Their own true hearts and dauntless arms
Have covered them with glory;
And while a Southerner treads the soil
They live in song and story.

Miss Irene Seymour Dickson of New Orleans,
Louisiana. In 1911 the 16 year old won the U.D.C.'s
Alison Medal for writing the best essay on the
"Causes of the War."

INSCRIPTION ON A CONFEDERATE MONUMENT

Fate denied them victory,
But crowned them
With glorious immortality.

A STATUE

A statue, proof of thy maker's art, bronze cast;
In days to come a monument to ages that have passed;
To-day to us who gather here
You are that someone our hearts hold dear.
Thy father, brother, husband, lover
At peace with God beneath the sod,
Who heard the call, who walked the way,
That soldier of right who wore the gray.

A statue mutely telling the sad story
Of a nation that died 'midst a halo of glory;
Of shattered hopes, ambitions dead,
Of noble blood that was freely shed;
Of the bugle's call for more to fall;
Of those who went, none being sent;
Of where the fiercest waxed the fray
Was found the soldier who wore the gray.

A statue linking the heavens with the earth,
The form of that hero to whom our nation gave birth,
Who followed on where honor led,
Till he rested with our holy dead;
And when at the last the trumpet's blast
Sends forth that call that comes to all.
As an honor guard on that last day
We'll find the soldier who wore the gray.[201]

HARRY T. HARRISON, 1908

INSCRIPTION ON A CONFEDERATE MONUMENT

They gave their lives for us,
For the honor of Alabama,
For the rights of the States,
And for the principles of the Union
As they were handed down to us
By the Fathers of our common country.

Michiganders flying the Confederate Battle Flag in 1907.

INSCRIPTION ON A CONFEDERATE MONUMENT

"The manner of their death was
The crowning glory of their lives."
Jefferson Davis

INSCRIPTION ON A CONFEDERATE MONUMENT

When marble wears away
And monuments are dust
The Songs that guard our soldiers' clay
Will fulfill their trust.

Miss Decca Lamar West, Confederate
Sponsor for Texas Division, U.C.V., 1907.

NOT ONE DROP OF BLOOD

Gazing reverently back to-day through the softening light of the
sleeping years, I declare to you that not one drop of blood was
shed in vain. Not one from that fateful morning at Sumter to
the sorrowful close at Appomattox. Peace with honor must pay
its price, be it life itself, and it is because the South paid that
price with prodigal hand that she stands erect among the
nations, catching upon her majestic brow the radiance of the
morning light.[202]

UNKNOWN

A 1921 magazine ad for the McNeel Marble Company of Marietta, Georgia, billed as "The South's Largest Monument Works."

APPENDIX A

SCULPTORS, DESIGNERS, & BUILDERS

SOME OF THE MEN & WOMEN ARTISTS BEHIND THE CONFEDERATE MONUMENTS IN THIS BOOK

Note: Though some of these individuals were Southerners, and even former Confederate soldiers, most were Europeans (mainly from France and Italy). A few Canadian and Yankee artists also appear in this list.

Alexander C. Doyle
John Roy
Frederick Wellington Ruckstuhl
M. J. L. Fougerousse
Charles Henry Niehaus
B. C. Alsup
Pompeo Coppini
Frank Teich
Otto Zirkel
Casper Buberl
Giuseppe Moretti
Edward Virginius Valentine
Antonin Mercie
Robert Reid

George Julian Zolnay
I. W. Durham
O. C. Connor
Virginia Montgomery
Moses Ezekiel
Antoine Durenne
Gutson Borglum
Augustus Lukeman
Walker Hancock
Roy Faulkner
Frederick William Sievers
J. Maxwell Miller
Herbert Barbee
Lewis Albert Guarbood

Famed sculptor George Julian Zolnay at work at the Tennessee Centennial Exposition, 1897.

APPENDIX B

ADDRESS AT THE FRANKLIN, TENNESSEE, CONFEDERATE MONUMENT DEDICATION

NOVEMBER 30, 1899

T he occasion which brings you here is one to which we have all looked forward with interest. We are making history to-day. *Future generations will point back with pride to this day—that their fathers and mothers, thirty-five years after the close of one of the bloodiest wars of history, when all passion had subsided, all animosities had been buried, and all sections of our common country were at peace with each other as brothers, had paid this tribute of affection to the memory of their countrymen.* A generation has passed, and this is in part the work of a new generation. *The corner stone of this monument is love—every rock in its foundation is cemented in love; every stroke of the chisel that worked out its beautiful symmetry was made in love; love, pure and simple, welled up in grateful hearts, as a token of which we transmit this monument to posterity.*

Confederate monument, Franklin, Tennessee. (Photo Lochlainn Seabrook)

This is the work of the noble women of Williamson County. They are the daughters of those women who near forty years ago gave such impetus to the cause of the Confederacy. Go back in memory to the stirring days of 1861. The women were as active as the men. There was an invading army at our borders; nothing was left to be done but go. The women aroused an enthusiasm that brooked no opposition, and *be it said to the lasting credit of Williamson [County, Tenn.] that she put more men in the field than she had voters.* The wife to her husband, the mother to her boy, the sister to her brother, the maiden to her sweetheart—all said: "Go. God be with you till we meet again! Should the fate of war befall you, and should that banner around which cluster the bright hopes of the Confederacy go down, you shall ever live in the hearts of your countrymen." We saw them go. They were boys, the flower of the land. Amid the hardships and deprivations of camp life, the desolation of the battlefield, they knew that promise would be redeemed, and gathered strength and courage from the fact. That promise has been as sacred with the daughters as it was with the mothers.

Who first suggested this monument, and that it be placed on the public square? is a question that has been asked. No man or woman can claim the credit. *The sentiment that something should be done to show to coming ages that we who saw and knew the Confederate soldier honored and loved him was spontaneous, and had its origin in no single mind; and upon the idea that a monument to his memory was the proper means we were all unanimous.*

Some at first preferred the beautiful McGavock [Confederate] Cemetery, the gift of that venerable gentleman [the owner John W. McGavock] whose memory is lovingly cherished by every man, woman, and child in Williamson County. The locality, while sacred as the resting place of the hallowed bones of our heroes, was too far removed from daily public contact.

Some preferred the battlefield, in sight of the railroad, that strangers in passing might know that we honor our countrymen. But *we don't build it for strangers; we build it for our children. We teach our children patriotism, to love, honor, and defend the government under which we live; and in recent months children of Confederate soldiers, who revere the government, offered the opportunity, have proven themselves to be worthy sons of honored sires.* And all, with

Colonel John W. McGavock.

rare exceptions, gradually came to the conclusion that the public square was the place, *that our children might know by daily observation of this monument that their fathers and mothers regarded the Confederate soldier as the grandest character in all history.*

History has her heroes from the earliest age. They stand out upon her pages as beacon lights, and have ignited the chivalry in the soul of many a boy. But we did not see them; we read about them. The men who left their homes that they had not seen for four years and followed [Confederate Gen. John Bell] Hood out of Tennessee, when they so

John B. Hood, C.S.A.

plainly saw that the star of the Confederacy had begun to set, were heroes before whom, in our eyes, all others pale into comparative insignificance. The men who followed Lee from Richmond, when they could but see that his Appomattox was near, were men in whose fidelity and valor the gods delight. These men were Southerners, our own countrymen. Some of them were from Williamson County. Some of them are here to-day; some have passed over the river, and are resting under the shades of eternity, awaiting the coming of their comrades, which will be short. *These Confederate Veterans are the men we desire to honor. It is an honor to belong to the race that could produce them. Our children should know them, and the richest heritage we have to leave them is that their blood flows through their veins. Such is the sentiment that built this monument and located it where it is.*

Contrast for a moment their home-coming in 1865 with that of their sons [from the Spanish-American War] in 1899—you have just witnessed the latter, in the sentiment of which we all heartily join. Ragged, foot-sore, weary, desolation on all sides, burned cities and homes, wasted fields. There was no trumpet to herald their coming; the sound of their approaching footsteps wasted away in the surrounding stillness. . . . But their countrymen and their countrywomen gave them a greeting worth more than the evanescent, fickle "*Io triumphe*" of the returning conqueror. With a silent, melancholy joy you met them; with outstretched arms and hearts full of love you received them, and showed to them then, as you have shown to the world for the thirty-five years since then, that you were proud of the record they made.

Only a few words in regard to the manner in which the money was raised. It is the work of the women of Williamson County. They have commanded the willing services of the men, and we have come and gone at their bidding.

The monument fund was started by a few women about fourteen years ago, and their number was continually increased. By ice cream suppers, concerts, cake walks, etc., from time to time a few dollars were raised. During this period these women devoted much of their attention to raising funds for needy Confederate soldiers, for the Soldiers' Home, McGavock Cemetery, etc. On this account the completion of the monument was deferred, and not for lack of interest in it. They succeeded in raising nearly $500. In 1896 Chapter No. 14. United Daughters of the Confederacy, was organized at Franklin, of which the most of these women became members. The chapter took charge of the enterprise, and went to work with a determination that saw nothing but success, and you see the result. While our pride in our soldiers is great, it is not greater than that we have in these women. *All praise to the United Daughters of the Confederacy! All praise to the women of Williamson County! It took just such women as we have to make the Confederate soldier what he was.*

Caroline "Carrie" E. McGavock (née Winder) of Carnton Plantation, Franklin, Tennessee, wife of John W. McGavock, the couple who donated the land on which the McGavock Confederate Cemetery now sits.

Donations have come to them from all sources. Democrats, Republicans, Populists, Prohibitionists, vied with each other in their contributions. School children gave their dimes. *Federal soldiers took stock, and this is the gift of all conditions of life, to stand as a monument of the affection of a grateful people.* While many Confederate soldiers have been liberal in their donations, I for one, have thought that we should not require much of them, because this is done not by them, but for them; it is done in their honor.

While history for a season may be colored by the conquerors, and thus shadow the truth, in time it will right itself, and the world will know, as we now know, that no age or country has ever produced the superior of our countrymen in courage, fidelity, and nobleness of character, and we wish to offer for coming generations our humble testimony of these virtues.

A monument in honor of the Confederate soldier, or something that will impress my children with the grandeur of his character, has been the

J. H. Henderson.

burden of my heart ever since I have had children. Now that it is an accomplished fact, no man can be more rejoiced.

On the fateful field of Franklin, in addition to the great fatality in the ranks, there was unprecedented fatality among the officers. They led their men. Six generals, one major general, and five brigadiers dead upon the field, and as many wounded. [Patrick Ronayne] Cleburne, [John] Adams, [John Carpenter] Carter, [Hiram Bronson] Granbury, [States Rights] Gist, and [Otho French] Strahl—*names that will ever be sacred to Southerners, as brave and as heroic as any in all the annals of history.*[203] — J. H. HENDERSON

Grave of Confederate General John Carpenter Carter, Rose Hill Cemetery, Columbia, Tennessee, who died on December 10, 1864, of wounds received at the Battle of Franklin II, November 30, 1864. (Photo Lochlainn Seabrook)

INSCRIPTION ON A CONFEDERATE MONUMENT

Never braver bled for brighter land,
Nor brighter land had a cause so grand.

APPENDIX C

ADDRESS AT FRANKLIN, TENNESSEE, DECORATION OF CONFEDERATE GRAVES AT MCGAVOCK CONFEDERATE CEMETERY

CIRCA 1901

Ladies, Gentlemen, Comrades, Daughters and Sons of the Soldiers of the South, we have met here to-day to reverence and honor our departed heroes, who have passed over the river, and are resting under the shade of the trees, waiting for us.

We have met not only to cherish their memories, but to vindicate their characters and the purity of their motives. *In 1861 the Southern people were the best informed, the most energetic, the most religious, and the most democratic people upon the earth. And I can also truthfully state that the people of the South were more attached to the Union as it existed under the Constitution than were the people of the North.* We were learned in agriculture, law, medicine, the literature of the Jews, Greeks, Romans, French, and English, and surpassed all others in statecraft. Our young men would gladly listen for hours to the discussion of political questions.

Our institution of slavery had partly separated us from other nations. *The Southern people were mostly descended from the soldiers of the revolution. Almost every Southern soldier could remember that his ancestors fought in the war of the revolution [1775], the war of 1812, the Indian wars [1812-1821], or the war with Mexico [1846-1848]. We had devised, framed, and fashioned the Union, and added to it all of its grandeur and glory. We had extended its boundaries from Virginia to California, and hence were attached to it.*

The young people may ask: Why did these heroes who sleep in their graves before us willingly offer up their lives? Why did they seek to dissolve the Union they had loved so much? The whole story can be told in a few minutes: As we understood it in 1861, and as our departed comrades understood it, with their parting words they urged us to be true and faithful.

When we gained our independence [from Britain in 1776] we were thirteen separate and distinct colonies. A more perfect Union was formed. The Constitution was the written contract entered into. The first trouble came during the war of 1812, when *the North*, in convention [of Liberals] at Hartford, Conn., *asserted the right of secession, and threatened to withdraw from the Union*, and make an ignoble peace with England. The next trouble came when Congress imposed a tariff for the declared purpose of protecting the manufactories of the North. John C. Calhoun requested that the acknowledged purpose be expressed in the act; so that its constitutionality could be tested in the Supreme Court of the United States. When this was refused he asserted that there was a tribunal of last resort—the people of the States. This was called "Nullification." *The North was the first to assert the right of secession; the South first to assert the right of nullification. Our rights in slaves were declared protected by the Constitution, the acts of Congress, and the decision of the Supreme Court of the United States. The North became "nullifiers," and a majority of the [Liberal] Northern States, through their Legislatures, nullified the Constitution, the acts of Congress, and the decision of the Supreme Court, and became the advocates of nullification.* In the midst of these disagreements, secret societies in the North collected, armed, and equipped a band of [Left-wing] men, who, with John Brown as their leader, invaded Virginia. These men were captured, convicted, and executed. Though they were guilty of treason and murder, the North threatened the South with vengeance for executing the law. *The Republican [then the Liberal party] or abolition party had been teaching the doctrine of secession and nullification, and had been vigorously enforcing the doctrine of nullification; but when it elected a President, the whole tone of the party changed.*

Looking down the length of McGavock Confederate Cemetery, Franklin, Tennessee, where nearly 1,500 Confederate soldiers are buried. (Photo Lochlainn Seabrook)

The [Conservative] South having been driven in desperation to resort to secession, the abolition party of the North became at once a great Union party. Their [Liberal] President, Mr. Lincoln, was a wise, shrewd, and cunning politician, with many virtues. Under his lead his party was taught that henceforth nothing but the preservation of the Union was to be taught and urged. He at once pacified the Democratic party of the North by bestowing offices and declaring that he sought nothing but the preservation of the Union. He raised a great army, but this army was not to turn its arms against the nullifiers of the North, but the secessionists of the South. The South remembered the John Brown raid and his intention as expressed in his code of laws, and *it was the universal opinion of the South that the raid of John Brown was but the advance guard of the Northern armies.* And thus this great war was begun. No power upon the earth could prevent it. No individual should be held responsible for what happened. Grim-visaged war ruled supreme. *We would have the young of this age and future ages understand what we thought and how we felt. How could we trust the promises of the [Liberal] North as long as their acts of nullification remained upon their statute books? How could we trust them when they raised armies to coerce us into obedience, and openly refused themselves to be bound by the Constitution, the acts of Congress, and the opinion of the Supreme Court?*

We did not fully understand what the negroes would do, or how they would act. *The North had brought them from Africa in their ships, and had sold them in the South, and now proposed to release them and place them in power over the white people of the South. This must have been prompted by the blindest prejudice and a most malignant heart or ignorance of the true philosophy of the situation. The South had done more for the negro than all the North put together. We had civilized and Christianized 4,000,000 of that race. Be it said to the honor of the women of the South: They had looked after the physical and spiritual welfare of the negro, and had so Christianized him and so attached him to his home that he was true and faithful in the hour of our greatest need, and many anticipated evils [such as slave uprisings and riots] did not come.*

To fully understand the Southern soldier, we must look at these things as we understood them in 1861. The North placed 2,500,000 soldiers in the field. The largest, the best-equipped and best-disciplined army of modern times; perhaps the world had never before seen such an army. This army was composed in part of the flower of the North, and all Europe was open to draw upon for soldiers, money, and all the sinews of war. The South had only 600,000 soldiers, no ships or arms, no money, and no friends. But we continued the unequal contest for four long years under countless disadvantages and deprivations.

There were no classes in the South; all white men were free and equal. In that grand army of the South the farmer, the planter, the mechanic, the merchant, the rich and the poor stood side by side upon terms of perfect equality—one in love and friendship. The boy of seventeen stood shoulder to shoulder with the man of sixty, and the boy was required to assume the responsibilities and perform the duties of a man. If those who sleep before us could come from their graves and appear before us as they appeared upon this bloody battlefield, you would be amazed at the great number of boys from seventeen to twenty years of age.

The brave never die in vain. The courage of the South had much to do with the preservation of local self-government and the individual rights of man. Happy must be the souls of our departed comrades who died for what has

Historical marker at the entrance of McGavock Confederate Cemetery, Franklin, Tennessee. (Photo Lochlainn Seabrook)

been called the "lost cause" when they look down upon us and see that, by wisdom, courage, patience, endurance, and devotion to law and order, we have gained the victory, and to know that *the whole civilized world gives more honor and praise to the vanquished than to the victors.*

We stand among the graves of our departed comrades who gave their lives for their country [at the Battle of Franklin II] on the 30th day of November, 1864. They come from all the States of our dear and beautiful South, and now rest with us. Some had come from Germany, Scotland, and Ireland to make their homes in the South. They have erected their own monuments, more durable than marble or brass. *They have made their names immortal.* We will decorate their graves. Upon one we will place the corn flower in honor of the place of his birth among the vine-clad hills of the Rhine, and with it we will place the magnolia in memory of the State of his adoption. Upon some we will place the lily, and upon some the shamrock, and upon all the beautiful and fragrant flowers of the South. You Daughters of the South will care for their graves, and will *cherish their virtues and deeds in your hearts forever.* Let us not forget to ever bear in kindly and honorable remembrance that peerless Southern gentleman, Col. John McGavock, now departed, and his noble wife (Caroline), who so generously gave this resting place for our dead in this most beautiful spot.[204] —JUDGE H. H. COOK

Another view of the McGavock Confederate Cemetery, Franklin, Tennessee; this one with the McGavocks' Confederate home, Carnton Plantation, in the background. (Photo Lochlainn Seabrook)

APPENDIX D

ADDRESS AT THE PARIS, TENNESSEE, CONFEDERATE MONUMENT DEDICATION

OCTOBER 13, 1900

You speak to posterity through this marble in a language commemorative of the heroism, of the soldiers of Henry County. At the same time you illustrate your own admiration for devotion to duty under circumstances of the greatest trial. The war between the States was not promoted by the men of Henry County. They were *conservative* and peaceful. War to them was terrible to contemplate, but they were not afraid of it or of its sacrifices. "They loved peace as they abhorred pusillanimity, but not peace at any price. There is a peace more destructive of the manhood of living men than war is destructive of his material body. Chains are worse than bayonets." The men of Henry were the sons and grandsons of Virginia and North Carolina. Their ancestors fought at Yorktown and King's Mountain, and were with [Andrew] Jackson at New Orleans. They had heard the stories of these great events from the pioneers, and were familiar with the trials and hardships of the cheerless days of the American revolution. They had learned that in a republic the liberty of the citizen and his rights of property must be asserted in the courts of the country, or at the ballot box, and failing here, a resort to arms was the logical consequence.

Tennessee declared at an early day, months before her own formal withdrawal from the Union, that *if the rule of force was applied to one State it would be accepted by her people as an act of war. The people of the South are and were a homogeneous race. A common ancestry with customs and institutions alike created a brotherhood stronger than the Union of States.* So when President Lincoln called for troops and inaugurated war against South Carolina and other seceding States there was no delay nor hesitation, no postponement for advice from leaders. The men of Henry upon their own motion rushed to arms. This action was a response to the lesson evolved from their education; a sense of duty controlled them; their judgments and hearts approved it, and before God and the tribunal of history we have no apology to offer. *We made our history honestly and conscientiously and we will write it truthfully as we made it, the protest of the Grand Army of the Republic [former Yankee solders] to the contrary notwithstanding. We want no accommodating committee to compromise our history, or to sugarcoat facts unpalatable to the sensibilities of men who will not accord honesty of purpose to the men of the South. We want posterity to know how our history was made; that it was done deliberately and voluntarily, and that we put our lives and fortunes to the touchstone of battle, and thus gave to the world the highest evidence of our sincerity.* Henry County furnished a larger

number of soldiers for the war, in proportion to white population, than any county in the State. They were earnest, brave men, full of dash and steadiness, responsive to discipline, with wonderful power to overcome fatigue and to resist the rigor of winter and the heat of summer. Meager rations were accepted without complaint: our surroundings were appreciated by all. There was no hope of foreign assistance, and no expectation of success unless it could be won on the battlefield. *The [U.S.] Federal Government had men, money, and munitions of war, and there was no limit to the supply. The Confederate States did not have a current dollar; when a soldier was killed or disabled there was no one to take his place. When a Federal soldier met the same fate a dozen recruits were sent forward.* The Army of Tennessee killed and disabled more men of Sherman's army than we had on our muster rolls, yet Sherman was stronger in numbers when he reached Atlanta than when he moved against Rocky Face Ridge one hundred days before that date, after fighting a battle almost every day. *No recruits came to the Confederates; there was no nation nor people upon whom we could call for help; ours was the orphan nation of the world, poor, naked, and hungry. As time passed hardships multiplied; the clothing of the men and the rations upon which they were fed were growing lighter in weight; ammunition was no longer abundant; the country was exhausted; pinching cold and hunger and poverty were in every household.*

To these conditions we at last succumbed. The men of Henry stood by the flag to the last: they participated in every battle of the Southwest. From Belmont to Bentonville they fell "on the red sand of the battlefield with bloody corpses strewn," and hundreds of them sleep in unmarked graves, but they are not forgotten. The stars may go down, but there is no oblivion for good or brave deeds.[205] — JAMES D. PORTER, FORMER TENNESSEE GOVERNOR & ADJUTANT GENERAL ON THE STAFF OF CONFEDERATE GENERAL BENJAMIN F. CHEATHAM

Confederate monument, Augusta, Georgia.

INSCRIPTION ON A CONFEDERATE MONUMENT

They died for the principles
Upon which all true republics
Are founded.

At the call of patriotism and duty,
They encountered the perils of the field.
And were faithful unto death.

They fought for conscience's sake,
And died for right.

APPENDIX E

EXTRACTS FROM THE ADDRESS AT THE GAINESVILLE, TEXAS, CONFEDERATE MONUMENT DEDICATION

JUNE 3, 1908

Our devotion to the South embraces those who maintained her birthright—*constitutional liberty*. Our reverence for Southern history extends to those who wrote in sacrificial blood the record of the war between the States. Our enthusiasm in glorious memories includes those who made the memories possible!

Our perpetuation of all this in stone finds expression in the heroic form of a Confederate soldier invoking the judgment of God upon our sacred cause, *the cause of right against might!*

In the sixties the mission of woman was to inspire. Now the mission of woman is to commemorate, and in commemorating *inspire future generations to be like the mothers of the South, like the veterans of the South!*

In the sixties woman wove the gray uniform and kissed the patriot sword that would defend home and children. Now she plants flowers on Confederate graves and establishes Confederate homes.

In the sixties woman by sacrifice and practical management made possible the maintenance of an army to defend country and rights. Now by sacrifice and practical management she makes possible the erection of monumental stones that perpetuate the principles for which that army fighting died or fighting lived and endured.[206] — MRS. J. M. WRIGHT

APPENDIX F

CONCERNING THE DEDICATION OF THE CONFEDERATE MONUMENT TO PRESIDENT JEFFERSON DAVIS, RICHMOND, VIRGINIA

JUNE 3, 1907

The dedication of the Davis monument was all that could have been imagined. Such a sea of human beings was hardly ever seen in the South, and for a Confederate occasion its like is not expected to appear again. The order of exercises was carried through as perfectly as could have been anticipated. Of course it was not expected that the  human voice could be heard by the vast throng, and without seeming impropriety a fine band of music played and hundreds of girls sang about the area of the monument. Such a joyous throng of so great magnitude must have rarely ever been witnessed on this earth.

Among all in that vast throng, met to give honor to the memory of the President of the Confederacy, but one spirit seemed dominant,—the love of the South, her heroes, her institutions, and the cause for which her sons fought and bled. While this day seemed one of joy, it was only such joy as comes to those who have faith in a cause . . . and glory in doing honor to those who bore the grievous burdens of our Southland in the bitter days that felt the hand of the invader. — BETTIE A. C. EMERSON

THOUGH MEN DESERVE, THEY MAY NOT WIN SUCCESS;
THE BRAVE WILL HONOR THE BRAVE, VANQUISHED NONE THE LESS.
(FROM THE TITLE PAGE OF *CONFEDERATE VETERAN*)

APPENDIX G

SPEECH DELIVERED AT THE UNVEILING OF THE STATUE OF JEFFERSON DAVIS IN NATIONAL STATUARY HALL, THE CAPITOL, WASHINGTON, D.C.

JUNE 2, 1931

The mighty figure represented in that beautiful bronze statue is to-day as much the idol of his people as he was their leader through the tragic days of his eventful career. He lived in a great epoch, and his name is blended with its glories and achievements, its reverses and disappointments. His was a colorful life, a life that was in conflict from youth to manhood and from manhood to the grave. He saw armies sweep illustrious battle fields, and became a captive; he was proclaimed at the head of a government, and stood accused in the courts of treason; he governed millions, and was imprisoned in a dungeon; he was crowned with coronets, and chained in irons; he pardoned thousands, but was denied one unto himself; under him a section stood steadfast, and in him sacrifice became supreme; he created a nation, and died a disfranchized citizen. No man was ever so loved and hated, exalted and excoriated, praised and condemned. Amid the storms of controversy and the fogs of dissension, his mighty figure arose majestically above all the rest. There never was a doubt as to where he stood on any question, and, when once his conclusions were formed, no power could move him from his position. To his teachings his people subscribed, and unto his care his section placed its keeping.

A graduate of West Point, he was highly educated and trained to discipline. His constant study and exceptional memory made his mind a storehouse of ready information. Grounded in the fundamental principles of government, groomed in the traditions of the Fathers, and inspired by the teachings of [Thomas] Jefferson and [John C.] Calhoun, he was an aggressive advocate and a dangerous antagonist. He never sought a conflict nor shirked one. A clear and forceful speaker, he never approached a subject but that he exhausted it. He was a devout Christian, but hated religious intolerance. There was no duplicity in his makeup. He detested hypocrisy and loathed deception. Demagogy to him was despicable. He spurned pretense and despised sham. Candor, courage, and conviction were the dominating qualities of his matchless character. Truly, what he said of [U.S. President] Franklin Pierce applied most fittingly to himself:

> If treachery had come near him, it would have stood abashed in the presence of his truthfulness, his manliness, and his confiding simplicity.

Small circumstances ofttimes influence the life of men and change the course of civil governments. History tells us that John Hampden and Oliver Cromwell once engaged passage to America; that George Washington almost became a mid-shipman in the British Navy. If Lincoln, when he left Kentucky, had gone to Mississippi, and Davis to Illinois, no one can vision what different circumstances might have surrounded their names.

> Fame unrecorded still is fame,
> Truth though unknown is truth the same;
> For the grandest glory known to man is heroism,
> Though it win no victor's wreath or Conqueror's crown.

Sixty-six years ago this Hall, made sacred by the legislative scenes of a Nation's progress and historic by the eloquence of her distinguished orators, was designated as Statuary Hall—our national Hall of Fame. The President of the United States [Ulysses S. Grant], by legislative mandate, was requested to invite all the States of the Union to place herein statues of their two most distinguished and illustrious characters.

What a conception! Parties may come and parties may go, administrations may rise and fall, but never, when all the States shall have accepted the invitation, will the membership of this exalted assembly change. They are and will be the marble and bronze figures of eminent and renowned citizens, warriors, scientists and statesmen, whose luminous deeds are the priceless heritages of a great and united country.

In all the reaches of the earth there is no place just like it. The number is limited, and those who climb the heights to reach it will compose a galaxy of jeweled characters, unrivaled by any other assembled group in all the world. Students of history and lovers of our country, through generations yet unborn, will visit here or read of those illustrious characters that have molded American history and shaped her course in every epoch of her journey. What a galaxy of stars to brighten the firmament of the past and light the Nation's future!

Unveiling ths statue of Jefferson Davis, National Statuary Hall, the Capitol Building, Washington, D.C., June 2, 1931.

The delay occasioned by Mississippi in accepting at this date the invitation of which she to-day avails herself has been due neither to lack of program nor enthusiasm upon her part. There has never been a day since she received the Nation's gracious invitation when the slightest doubt was entertained that her first choice, among all her array of distinguished and illustrious characters, to occupy a place here would be

Jefferson Davis. No other name is so closely interwoven with her history and so securely riveted in the affections of her people. Without apology for the part she played in that tragic drama which divided the sections and tore the Nation asunder, she has realized the sensitive character of the national situation, and believed that in the passing of the years the scars of strife and the wounds of conflict would heal and the time would come when the tolerant spirit of a reunited people would concede to the people of both sections a conscientious discharge of duty as they saw it under the Constitution and principles of our government.

Mr. Davis had been their inspiration and hope, their leader and vicarious sufferer. It was he, above all the rest, who, during that stormy epoch preceding the war, gave expression to their feelings. It was he who, when the crisis came, was the unanimous choice of his section as head and leader. It was he who, when the war drums throbbed no longer and the battle flags were furled, walked down the long vista to the end of life, carrying the alleged sins of his section, without stooping his shoulders or bowing his head.

Mississippi has believed that the time was inevitable when a just Nation would refuse to measure one citizen by one standard and all others who believed and acted as he did by another standard. She has believed that a just country would not hold one man accountable for that which all others had been forgiven. She has believed that the healing process of time would reveal nothing more in the utterances and deportment of Mr. Davis than could be found in the utterances and deportment of tens of thousands of others. She has believed that they would in time realize that the principles advocated by him met the approval of Southern leaders, and that his every act was enthusiastically acclaimed in the burning heart of his section. She has believed that as the people of other sections became more familiar with his character and record they would say, as [Confederate General] Ben [Jefferson] Hill said of him: "He was the most honest, the truest, the bravest, the tenderest, and the manliest man I ever knew."

When that martial and stately figure of [Confederate General] Robert E. Lee was placed by Virginia in this rotunda, it was the beginning of finer feeling between the sections; when Alabama selected that heroic figure of [Confederate General] Joe Wheeler to occupy a place of honor in this historic Hall, it kindled still warmer fires of common understanding. When Florida answered her invitation with a salute to [Confederate General] Edmund Kirby Smith, it was a rebel yell for a common country. When Georgia graced this Hall with the figure of Alexander H. Stephens, a further step was taken in the cementing process of the two sections.

And to-day, as Mississippi places her two illustrious and matchless military geniuses, statesmen, and leaders in this Hall, the last link is forged in the chain that will forever hold our country together.

Amid the rivalries, jealousies and cross-currents of conflict and controversy, it is always difficult to make a true estimate of one's life and character. We must draw ourselves away from the picture, that we may catch a better vision of its delicate nature and fine parts, and, in the passing of years, as generations travel farther away from the tragic scenes of the sixties, the qualities of Mississippi's beloved statesman and the South's illustrious leader will become more appreciated and fixed.

Few men in the history of the Nation rendered more signal service for the country in peace and in war than did Mr. Davis. As a young army officer, fresh from West Point, he displayed such military instinct and superiority that he was intrusted with responsible commands in carrying the flag into the great Northwest, subduing war like Indians, and opening up posts for our trade and commerce. Even though called by his people to serve as a Representative of his State in this very Hall, when the country was threatened and the war clouds gathered, he immediately resigned his seat in this body [June 1846], returned to the State he loved, and led his regiment of Mississippi volunteers to heights of glory upon the cactus plains of Mexico. No officer of the American army ever displayed more superb military genius and greater courage than did Mr. Davis in the service of his country in the Mexican War. In the military records of this country are written his matchless deeds and unrivaled exploits to his credit and the glory of his country.

Mr. [William Hickling] Prescott, the historian, in speaking of his services in the Senate, said that though he served with [Daniel] Webster, Calhoun, [Henry] Clay, and [Thomas Hart] Benton, and other great intellects, "[Davis] was the most accomplished member of that body." Mr. Redpath said of him that "he was a statesman with clean hands and a pure heart, who served his people faithfully and well from budding manhood to hoary age, without thought of self, to the best of his ability."

As Secretary of War for four years [under U.S. President Franklin Pierce], he placed the preparedness of this country on a basis of leadership and efficiency unapproached before. His constructive qualities of statesmanship, his candor in giving advice without attempt to please or flatter, his knowledge of men and questions, made him a pillar of strength to Franklin Pierce, and won for him the highest encomiums as Secretary of War.

As we to-day pay this deserved tribute to his character and worth, we might recall that when this old Hall was abandoned and the new and more modern wings planned construction, the Congress, by joint resolution, took from another department of the government the supervision of the construction of these additions and placed the work in the hands of Mr. Davis, then Secretary of War, so impressed were they with his honesty, fairness and executive ability.

Inscription on a Confederate soldier's gravestone. (Photo Lochlainn Seabrook)

And so it is fitting that here in this Nation's Capitol, in which he played such a commanding part, this beautiful bronze statue should be placed in tribute to his illustrious achievements and mighty character. How well he adorns it! He is not among strangers; there are his comrades of the South—Lee, [Confederate General Wade] Hampton, Wheeler, Stephens, Kirby Smith, and [Confederate officer] James Zachariah George. With them he scaled the heights of victory and retreated down the slopes of defeat. Over there are Clay, Webster, Benton, [Lewis] Cass, and Calhoun, his idol, with whom he served in the Senate of the United States. Those men all, whether divided upon the battle grounds of debate or united upon the battlefields of war, are entitled to their places here, fixed in the history of a great and reunited country.[207] — THE HONORABLE PAT HARRISON OF MISSISSIPPI

APPENDIX H

THE CONFEDERATE WOMEN OF NORTH CAROLINA GO UP AGAINST THE ANTI-SOUTH SENTIMENT OF THE U.S. GOVERNMENT SHORTLY AFTER LINCOLN'S WAR

WRITTEN SPRING 1895

Our women have always been active in advancing any good cause, and especially were they helpful in the dark trials during and directly after the war. The women of North Carolina were no exception to this rule, and by their untiring exertions have done much to keep alive the memory of those who so nobly sacrificed themselves upon the altar of their country.

The following extracts were made from a paper by Mrs. M. L. Shipp, in the woman's edition of the *News and Observer*, May 20, 1895, in regard to the most prominent association of the state:

"The Ladies' Memorial Association of Wake County was formed in 1865, when it was necessary to remove from the grounds of the Pettigrew Hospital the remains of the Confederate soldiers buried there. It was but a short while after the Federals took possession of Raleigh before the Mayor was notified that they admired the spot where rested the Confederate dead, and ordered that they be moved at once, or they would be thrown out in the country road. A town meeting was called, and the association formed, Mrs. Lawrence O'Bryan Branch being made President; Miss Sophia Partridge, Secretary; and Miss Annie Mason, Treasurer. The other charter members were Mrs. Henry Miller, Mrs. Lucy Evans, Mrs. Robert Lewis, Mrs. Mary Lacy, Vice-Presidents; Miss Margaret Iredell and Mrs. John Devereaux.

"A resting—place was selected for the reinterment of the beloved dead, and, with the help of the young men and boys of the town, the work was successfully accomplished. The graves were comparatively few at first, but none were safe from Sherman's 'bummers' [scavengers], as there was scarcely a new-made grave anywhere but what was opened by these men, in search of treasures; so it was a sacred trust, most religiously kept by the young men and women, to visit these graves almost daily and see that they were kept in order. The association grew in numbers and the interest increased. Many Confederate dead from the country were moved to this spot, and the grounds were laid off and improved by Serg. Hamilton, a soldier of the Confederate army who lost both eyes from a wound.

"After the death of Gen. Jackson the 10th of May had been selected as Memorial Day, when the citizens were to repair to the cemetery to participate in the services there. No procession was allowed unless the United States flag was carried, and as it was several years before the ladies were so much 'reconstructed' as to march under this flag, the gathering was without special order or ceremony. The services were very simple, but impressive in the stillness of the forest.

"To raise funds to care for the Confederate dead and erect a monument to their memory, every legitimate means was resorted to by the association. Many entertainments were given in town, and the young people would go to villages near the town and assist in giving entertainments there. This was not done without risk, as it was reported that contraband articles were for sale, such as Confederate flags, a strand of Gen. Lee's hair, pictures of President Davis or any Confederate general; so there would be the sudden appearance of a bluecoat with orders to search the room for these contraband articles. None were ever found, however, and the efforts of the ladies were so successful that they were able to raise funds sufficient, with appropriations from the state, to erect the monument now standing in the cemetery. By this time the town and state were in a measure relieved from martial law, and a fitting dedication was allowed.

"The Ladies' Memorial Association of Wake County is still in existence, and through its efforts not only the Confederate dead of North Carolina, but of other Southern states, have been brought from the field of Gettysburg and the United States burying-ground at Arlington, and now rest together in this cemetery. Through their efforts, also, the Home for Old Soldiers was secured, and after thirty years the state has honored her soldiers by placing a monument to their memory in the capitol grounds at Raleigh.

"The success and noble work of the association is mainly due to its first President, Mrs. Lawrence O'Bryan Branch, who so nobly put aside her own grief to care for those who, with her husband, had given their lives to the cause of truth and justice."[208] — MRS. M. L. SHIPP

Battle of Fort Sumter, April 12-14, 1861.

APPENDIX I

YANKS RETURN CAPTURED CONFEDERATE FLAGS OVER 60 YEARS AFTER THE WAR UNDER THE AUSPICES OF U.S. PRESIDENT CALVIN COOLIDGE

DECEMBER 12, 1927

Central figures of a group showing Confederate flags returned from the State of Maine to Virginia, North Carolina, and Texas, the formal ceremonies taking place in 1927 in Washington, D.C. Afterward the participants met with President Coolidge, who is in the center of the group, with Gen. Walker B. Freeman, of Virginia on the right.

Some interesting occasions have been recorded during the past several months when Confederate flags captured during the War between the States were returned by their captors after being held for over sixty years. Notable among these occasions was that ceremony in Washington D.C., when seven flags captured by a Maine regiment were returned to the States from whose troops they were taken. These flags had been stored in the State House at Augusta, Me., and by special resolution of the late encampment of the G.A.R. [Union veterans], the governor of that State was directed to return them. The ceremonies were carried out on the steps of the Capitol at Washington. Governor [Ralph Owen] Brewster, of Maine, with his staff, Commander Pillsbury, of the Maine G.A.R., and his staff, made up a fine looking body of men, bringing the old flags of Virginia, North Carolina, and Texas as representatives of the universal sentiment of the people of the Pine Tree State toward the States of the South, whose representatives were there in the same feeling of amity and good will. The flags of the Virginia troops were received by Gen. Walker Burford Freeman, of Richmond, former Commander in Chief, U.C.V. . . .

Following the brief ceremonies, which were witnessed by several cabinet officers, special representatives of the different States connected with the occasion, prominent members of the G.A.R. and U.C.V. [United Confederate Veterans] in uniform, the Confederate veterans called upon President [Calvin] Coolidge with their regained silken trophies, and were photographed with the President as the central figure.[209]

INSCRIPTION ON A CONFEDERATE MONUMENT

Would it not be
A shame for us,
If their memories part
From our land and heart,
And a wrong to them,
And a shame for us?

The glories they won
Shall not wane for us,
In legend and lay
Our heroes in gray
Shall forever live
Over again for us.

APPENDIX J

AMERICA'S NATIONAL CEMETERIES

CURRENT AS OF 1917

The following is a list of the National Cemeteries in the United States authorized by act of Congress of July 17, 1862, and subsequent acts, and shows the number of interments in each up to June 30, 1917. The list was taken from the *National Tribune*, of Washington, D.C., for which paper it was prepared by the War Department (Office of the Quartermaster General):

Alexandria, La: 4,542

Alexandria, Va: 3,565

Andersonville, Ga: 13,723

Andrew Johnson, Tenn: 19

Annapolis, Md: 2,544

Antietam, Md: 4,759

Arlington, Va: 24,478

Balls Bluff, Va: 25

Barrancas, Fla: 1 ,663

Baton Rouge, La: 3,163

Battle Ground, D.C.: 44

Beaufort, S.C.: 9,492

Beverly, N.J.: 201

Camp Butler, Ill: 1,597

Camp Nelson, Ky: 3,660

Cave Hill, Ky: 4,790

Chalmette, La: 13,120

Chattanooga, Tenn: 13,706

City Point, Va: 5,180

Cold Harbor, Va: 1,969

Corinth, Miss: 5,737

Crown Hill, Ind: 816

Culpeper, Va: 1,375

Custer Battle Field, Mont: 1,583

Cypress Hills, N.Y.: 7,673

Danville, Ky: 359

Danville, Va: 1,331

Fayetteville, Ark: 1,316

Finns Point, N.J.: 2,632

Florence, S.C.: 3,013

Fort Donelson, Tenn: 676

Fort Gibson, Okla: 2,488

Fort Harrison, Va: 818

Fort Leavenworth, Kan: 4,046

Fort McPherson, Nebr: 854

Fort Scott, Kan: 885

Fort Smith, Ark: 2,399

Fredericksburg, Va: 15,186

Gettysburg, Pa: 3,680

Glendale, Va: 1,198

Grafton, W. Va: 1 ,276

Hampton, Va: 11,549

Jefferson Barracks, Mo: 12,642

Jefferson City, Mo: 843

Keokuk, Iowa: 906

Knoxville, Tenn: 3,552

Lebanon, Ky: 875

Lexington, Ky: 1,136

Little Rock, Ark: 6,916

Loudon Park, Md: 4,002

Marietta, Ga: 10,424

Memphis, Tenn: 14,441

Mexico City, Mexico: 1,552
Mill Springs, Ky: 729
Mobile, Ala: 1,127
Mound City, Ill: 5,432
Nashville, Tenn: 16,77 1
Natchez, Miss: 3,414
New Albany, Ind: 3,146
Newbern, N.C.: 3,399
Philadelphia, Pa: 3,444
Poplar Grove, Va: 6,217
Port Hudson, La: 3,851
Quincy, Ill: 317
Raleigh, N.C.: 1,214
Richmond, Va: 6,578
Rock Island, Ill: 424
Salisbury, N.C.: 12,149

San Antonio, Tex: 1,970
San Francisco, Cal: 7,166
Santa Fe, N. Mex: 1,099
Seven Pines, Va: 1,400
Shiloh, Tenn: 3,622
Soldiers' Home, D.C.: 7,825
Springfield, Mo: 2,451
St. Augustine, Fla: 1,775
Staunton, Va: 766
Stone River, Tenn: 6,149
Vicksburg, Miss: 17,070
Wilmington, N.C.: 2,361
Winchester, Va: 4,546
Woodlawn, N.Y.: 3,278
Yorktown, Va: 2,196
TOTAL DEAD: 372,164

Over seventy thousand of these are Union soldiers who died in Confederate prisons and are buried in National Cemeteries adjacent to the points where the prisons were located. Andersonville, Florence, and Salisbury are entirely prison cemeteries. Of these interments approximately 10,578 are those of Confederates, being mainly in the following National Cemeteries:

Arlington, Va: 300
Camp Butler, Ill: 865
City Point, Va: 131
Cypress Hills, N.Y.: 456
Finns Point, N.J.: 2,436
Hampton, Va: 284
Fort Smith, Ark: 127
Jefferson Barracks, Mo: 826
Little Rock, Ark: 922
Philadelphia, Pa: 200
Springfield, Mo: 549
Woodlawn, N.Y.: 3,012
TOTAL CONFEDERATE DEAD: 10,108[210]

POEM TO THE CONFEDERATE SOLDIER

Sorrow and pain and anger,
Hatred and death are fled.
It is only glory lingers
With the great immortal dead.
For they knew defeat—whate'er it cost
Could never mean their cause was lost!

CIRCA EARLY 19ᵀᴴ CENTURY

"After war comes peace."

"Everyone should do all in his power to collect and disseminate the truth, in the hope that it may find a place in history and descend to posterity. . . . History is not the relation of campaigns and battles, and generals or other individuals, but that which shows the principles for which the South contended and which justified her struggle for those principles. . . . All that the South has ever asked or desired is that the Union founded by our forefathers should be preserved, and that the government as was originally organized should be administered in purity and truth."[211]

CONFEDERATE GENERAL ROBERT E. LEE

NOTES

1. Emerson, p. 15. Father Ryan's poem was without a title, so I gave it my own. Its appropriateness may be judged by the reader.

2. Woods, p. 47.

3. On Lincoln's socialistic, Marxist, and communist thoughts, ideas, and tendencies, see e.g., McCarty, passim; Browder, passim; Seabrook, LW, passim; Seabrook, AWAITBLA, passim; Seabrook, ALWALJDWAC, passim; Benson and Kennedy, passim.

4. See J. W. Jones, TDMV, pp. 144, 200-201, 273.

5. See Seabrook, TAHSR, passim. See also, Pollard, LC, p. 178; J. H. Franklin, pp. 101, 111, 130, 149; Nicolay and Hay, ALCW, Vol. 1, p. 627.

6. BISG (the "Book Industry Study Group"), for example—a Left-wing organization which describes itself as "the leading book trade association for standardized best practices, research and information, and events"—gives its BISAC ("Book Industry Standards and Communications") listing for works on the War for Southern Independence under the heading "Civil War Period, 1850-1877." Nearly all books published in the U.S.A. today are under the categorizational control of this Liberal group located in New York City.

7. See e.g., Seabrook, TQJD, pp. 30, 38, 76.

8. See e.g., J. Davis, RFCG, Vol. 1, pp. 55, 422; Vol. 2, pp. 4, 161, 454, 610. Besides using the term "Civil War" himself, President Davis cites numerous other individuals who use it as well.

9. See e.g., *Confederate Veteran*, March 1912, Vol. 20, No. 3, p. 122.

10. Minutes of the Eighth Annual Meeting, July 1898, p. 87.

11. Seabrook, AL, p. 516.

12. See my book of the same name.

13. *Confederate Veteran*, April 1911, Vol. 19, No. 5, p. 155.

14. Mish, s.v. "Americanism."

15. For a complete and detailed discussion of this topic, see Seabrook, ALWALJDWAC.

16. The three short portraits of Twain, Emerson, and Whitman that follow are not meant to cast aspersion on their characters. Indeed, in deference to their memories I have left out what many would consider the most damning and shocking facts surrounding their lives. Mention should also be made that all three possessed many positive traits as well, and that they made numerous contributions to American culture. Finally, it must be acknowledged that their views on many of the matters and issues referenced here changed over time. My sole purpose is to show that mainstream history, including American Civil War history, is seldom what one thinks it is.

17. Kaplan, MCAMT, pp. 168, 243, 255-256, 271-278, 296-297, 287, 325, 368. Note: Twain was known to his friends as "the most desouthernized Southerner" they had ever met. Kaplan, p. 196.

18. Seabrook, LW, p. 74.

19. Seabrook, LW, pp. 77-78.

20. Russell, pp. 38, 165, 173, 229, 264-265, 268, 305.

21. Seabrook, ARB, pp. 41-42.

22. By the modern Liberal mainstream's standards (which are the opposite of those still held in the traditional South), *Leaves of Grass* is quite tame. In fact, Whitman's non-traditional (some would say perverted) views, and many even far more extreme, are now routinely featured and promoted in popular culture (e.g., TV and film) and in our schools down to as young as elementary age—a direct result of America-hating, Liberal-run Hollywood and the radical anti-American Left that runs our school system. These, as well as many other progressives, are seeking the destruction of Americanism (conservatism) through the normalization of un-American, un-Christian, un-patriotic views and values.

23. Kaplan, WW, pp. 169-170, 211, 276, 291-292, 300.

24. Seabrook, TUCWQB, p. 56.

25. As mentioned above, none of this is meant to personally denigrate Twain, Emerson, or Whitman, three individuals who I have read widely, sometimes enjoyed, and even quote in my books. Rather, it is to demonstrate that just as nearly all mainstream biographies are fabricated, so is nearly all American Civil War history.

26. Seabrook, TGYC, p. 41.

27. Seabrook, CFF, p. 266. My emphasis.

28. Seabrook, CFF, p. 267. My emphasis.

29. Seabrook, CFF, p. 267. My emphasis.

30. Seabrook, CFF, p. 267. My emphasis.

31. See photo on page 180.

32. Seabrook, CFF, pp. 267-268.

33. My emphasis. Regulation 18 U.S.C. 1369 is in turn related to H.R. 2170, the "Veterans' Memorials Protection Act of 2003"; H.R. 2076, the "Veterans' Memorial Preservation and Recognition Act of 2003"; and H.R. 4527, the "Enhanced Protection of Our Cultural Heritage Act."

34. My emphasis. For more information, see *Federal Historic Preservation Laws: The Official Compilation of U.S. Cultural Heritage Statutes*, U.S. Department of the Interior, Washington, D.C., 2006. Also see the *Congressional Record*, available online at: https://www.congress.gov/congressional-record. For up-to-date information on these and other laws concerning the preservation of historic items (e.g., Confederate monuments), see Website: www.nps.gov/subjects/historicpreservation/laws.htm.

35. One of the facts most routinely disregarded by the anti-South movement is that many Confederate officers had served in the U.S. military prior to Lincoln's War, in particular fighting in the Mexican-American War (1846-1848). There are far too many to list here, but two of the most notable examples are Robert E. Lee and Stonewall Jackson, both who fought with distinction in that conflict as U.S. officers. Another example is Jefferson Davis; again, not only was he a U.S. officer in the Mexican-American War, he was also an antebellum U.S. Senator, a U.S. Representative, and U.S. Secretary of War (under U.S. President Franklin Pierce). Thus, even if the U.S. Congress did not recognize Confederate soldiers as U.S. military veterans (thankfully it does), Confederates like Davis, Lee, and Jackson certainly officially qualify as such. For this reason alone it is a crime to molest their memorials in any way.

36. Seabrook, VCP, p. 98.

37. Left-wing fantasies include the following: "All white people are racists"; Western culture is inherently evil"; "Conservatives are cruel, selfish, and greedy"; "Only Liberals truly care about the world, people, the environment"; *ad infinitum*.

38. Mish, s.v. "civil war."

39. For more on this topic, see Seabrook, C101, passim.

40. Seabrook, EYWTATCIW, pp. 23-25. For more on my personal views on the term "civil war," and also why I am sometimes forced to use it, see my "Notes to the Reader."

41. Washington did not become president until after the Revolutionary War. I list him here as the Commander-in-Chief of the Continental Army.

42. Seabrook, TQJD, p. 62. My emphasis.

43. Seabrook, AWAITBLA, p. 8. My emphasis.

44. Seabrook, AWAITBLA, p. 139. My emphasis.

45. Seabrook, AWAITBLA, p. 208. My emphasis.

46. For more on the Northern states' antebellum secession plans to form a "Northern Confederacy," see Seabrook, C101, and Seabrook, AL.

47. Seabrook, AWAITBLA, pp. 208-209. My emphasis.

48. I coined the word confederalism because there was no word in the English language that exactly describes the ideas behind confederate governments; that is, confederacies. Thus (borrowing various words and phrases from Webster), I define confederalism as the socially traditional and politically conservative philosophy, principles, and policies of the original American government, the confederate republic: a body of people, states, or countries united by a constitutionally-based league or compact, which possesses a small, weak, limited central government that rests on states' rights, and whose supreme power resides in the people, and whose states are free, independent, and sovereign.

49. Seabrook, AWAITBLA, pp. 254-255. My emphasis.

50. Seabrook, AWAITBLA, p. 255. My emphasis.

51. Emerson, pp. 261, 263. My emphasis.

52. *Confederate Veteran*, May 1930, Vol. 38, No. 5, p. 205. My emphasis.

53. Seabrook, AWAITBLA, p. 35. My emphasis.

54. For more on these topics, see Seabrook, AWAITBLA; Seabrook, LW.

55. Seabrook, AWAITBLA, passim.

56. Seabrook, EYWTATCWIW, pp. 33-37.

57. Seabrook, AWAITBLA, pp. 307-308. My emphasis.

58. Seabrook, LW, p. 50.

59. Seabrook, EYWTATCWIW, pp. 30, 36.

60. Seabrook, LW, pp. 15-65.

61. Seabrook, AWAITBLA, pp. 307-308. My emphasis.

62. Seabrook, AWAITBLA, pp. 307-308.

63. Seabrook, LW, pp. 16-17.

64. Seabrook, AWAITBLA, pp. 142-143.

65. Seabrook, LW, pp. 15-65.

66. Seabrook, LW, p. 17. My emphasis.

67. Seabrook, ALWALJDWAC, passim.

68. Seabrook, ALWALJDWAC, passim.

69. Seabrook, EYWTAASIW, passim; Seabrook, LW, passim.

70. Seabrook, AWAITBLA, pp. 58-60.

71. Seabrook, LW, passim.

72. Seabrook, RUACTB, pp. 504-505, 510, 515-516.

73. *Confederate Veteran*, April 1918, Vol. 26, No. 4, p. 143.

74. Seabrook, RUACTB, p. 249.

75. Seabrook, RUACTB, p. 317.

76. Seabrook, LW, p. 115.

77. *Confederate Veteran*, April 1918, Vol. 26, No. 4, pp. 143-144. My emphasis.

78. Seabrook, EYWTAASIW, pp. 47, 163, 182, 231, 420, 541, 647.

79. Seabrook, EYWTAASIW, pp. 48, 549, 550.

80. Seabrook, EYWTAASIW, pp. 549-645.

81. Seabrook, EYWTAASIW, pp. 220, 221, 270, 552, 553, 558-566, 569-570, 799.

82. Seabrook, EYWTAASIW, pp. 86-88.

83. Seabrook, EYWTAASIW, p. 245.

84. Seabrook, TUCWQB, p. 82.

85. Seabrook, EYWTAASIW, p. 426.

86. Seabrook, EYWTAASIW, pp. 441-443.

87. Seabrook, EYWTAASIW, pp. 459-513.

88. Seabrook, EYWTAASIW, pp. 236-242.

89. Seabrook, EYWTAASIW, pp. 62-119.

90. Chesnut was the husband of the celebrated Southern diarist Mary Boykin Chesnut.

91. Seabrook, EYWTAASIW, p. 428.

92. Seabrook, LW, p. 18.

93. Seabrook, RUACTB, pp. 473-474. My emphasis.

94. Seabrook, RUACTB, pp. 279-280.

95. Seabrook, EYWTAASIW, pp. 270, 426.

96. Seabrook, EYWTAASIW, pp. 47, 420, 424, 541, 647.

97. Seabrook, EYWTAASIW, pp. 167, 199, 225, 271, 541-542, 561-562, 569, 870.

414 ⌒ CONFEDERATE MONUMENTS

98. Seabrook, TCOTCSOAE, p. 65.

99. Seabrook, EYWTAASIW, pp. 242-244.

100. Seabrook, TGYC, pp. 132-133.

101. Seabrook, EYWTAASIW, pp. 736.

102. Seabrook, EYWTATCWIW, p. 165. In arriving at these figures, particularly those of African-Americans, I am using the definition of a "soldier" as established by German-American Union General August Valentine Kautz. In 1864 he wrote: "In the fullest sense, any man in the military service who receives pay, whether sworn in or not, is a soldier, because he is subject to military law. Under this general head, laborers, teamsters, sutlers, chaplains, etc., are soldiers." Seabrook, EYWTAASIW, p. 785.

103. Seabrook, EYWTATCWIW, p. 159. My emphasis.

104. *Confederate Veteran*, September 1915, Vol. 23, No. 9, p. 404.

105. Stonewall Jackson's army alone contained some 3,000 black Confederate soldiers. Seabrook, EYWTAASIW, p. 786.

106. Seabrook, AWAITBLA, passim.

107. Seabrook, EYWTAASIW, pp. 549-646.

108. Seabrook, EYWTATCWIW, pp. 199-202.

109. John 13:34.

110. For a detailed discussion on what I call the Reconstruction KKK, see Seabrook, NBFATKKK.

111. Seabrook, EYWTAASIW, pp. 660-661.

112. Seabrook, EYWTAASIW, p. 661. My emphasis. Note: My cousin Senator Hayne is not praising the institution of slavery, but rather the mild treatment of blacks under the Southern slavery system in comparison to the barbaric treatment they received under so-called "freedom" in the North.

113. Seabrook, EYWTAASIW, pp. 679-680.

114. *Confederate Veteran*, March 1897, Vol. 5, No. 3, p. 166.

115. Seabrook, AWAITBLA, pp. 187-190.

116. Seabrook, EYWTAASIW, p. 593.

117. Seabrook, EYWTAASIW, pp. 592-594.

118. Seabrook, EYWTATCWIW, p. 110.

119. Seabrook, EYWTATCWIW, pp. 113-114.

120. Seabrook, AL, pp. 29, 275, 293-318.

121. Seabrook, AL, p. 265.

122. Seabrook, AL, pp. 67-68. My emphasis.

123. Seabrook, TUAL, p. 28.

124. Seabrook, AL, p. 479, passim.

125. Seabrook, AL, p. 109. My emphasis.

126. See Seabrook, LW, passim; Seabrook AL, passim.

127. Seabrook, LW, p. 82.

128. Seabrook, RUACTB, pp. 148-149.

129. Seabrook, AL, p. 530.

130. *Confederate Veteran*, November 1896, Vol. 4, No. 11, p. 371.

131. Seabrook, AL, pp. 530-531, 535.

132. Seabrook, AL, p. 527.

133. Seabrook, LW, pp. 56-61.

134. Seabrook, RU, p. 269. My emphasis.

135. Seabrook, LW, pp. 36, 38-39, 41, 43, 78, 156-157.

136. Seabrook, AL, pp. 315, 320, 322, 326, 372.

137. Seabrook, AL, pp. 121, 128, 218.

138. It is well-known, for example, that Liberals only want open borders because they believe it will help ensure the illegal alien vote.

139. Seabrook, VCP, p. 422.

140. Seabrook, AL, pp. 132-133, 142, 254, 257, 318, 379, 477-479.

141. Seabrook, TUAL, p. 82.

142. Seabrook, TUAL, pp. 79-80.

143. Seabrook, TUAL, p. 99.

144. Seabrook, TUAL, p. 93.

145. Seabrook, EYWTAASIW, pp. 220-222.

146. Seabrook, EYWTAASIW, p. 221.

147. Seabrook, AWAITBLA, p. 149.

148. Seabrook, LW, passim.

149. Seabrook, RUACTB, pp. 283-284.

150. Seabrook, RUACTB, pp. 339-341.

151. Seabrook, RUACTB, p. 429.

152. For more on this general topic, see Seabrook, LW.

153. Seabrook, RUACTB, p. 351.

154. Seabrook, RUACTB, pp. 351-352.

155. For more on the Reconstruction period from the South's point of view, see Seabrook, AL; Seabrook, NBFATKKK; Seabrook, LW; Seabrook, TUC.

156. Seabrook, AWAITBLA, p. 85.

157. Seabrook, LW, p. 306.

158. For more on Lincoln's War from the Southern perspective, see Seabrook, EYWTATCWIW; Seabrook, LW; Seabrook, TGYC; Seabrook, GTBTAY; Seabrook, TUC; Seabrook, RUACTB; Seabrook, AWAITBLA; Seabrook, AL; Seabrook, TGYC.

159. Seabrook, ARB, p. 312.

160. Seabrook, TUCWQB, p. 43.

161. Seabrook, RUACTB, p. 387.

162. Seabrook, TQREL, p. 156.

163. Seabrook, TQREL, p. 163.

164. Seabrook, TQREL, p. 167.

165. Seabrook, TQREL, p. 213.

166. Seabrook, TQREL, pp. 206, 207.

167. Seabrook, RUACTB, p. 47. My emphasis.

168. Captured in battle by Union troops during Lincoln's War, the Confederate flags had recently been kindly returned to the South by several Northern states. South-loathers, of course, responded to this charitable gesture with anger and hate, for it aids the Liberal cause to keep the two sections on hostile terms.

169. Prior to becoming president, Wilson taught history at two of America's most liberal schools: Bryn Mawr and Princeton.

170. See Appendix B. For more on the topic of this paragraph, see Seabrook, RUACTB, p. 496.

171. Emerson, pp. 267-268.

172. See Seabrook, C101, passim.

173. Seabrook, RUACTB, p. 238.

174. Gallison, p. 29. My emphasis.

175. O'Ferrall, p. 149.

176. *Confederate Veteran*, June 1898, Vol. 6, No. 6, p. 253. My emphasis.

177. There is no disguising the fact that the ultimate goal of liberalism is socialism, and that the ultimate goal of socialism is communism: thanks to the thorough work of left-wing teachers and professors, at least 70 percent of Americans under 25, the new generation now coming into power, identify themselves as "socialists." This is the same evil that Confederate soldiers (Conservatives) fought against in 1861.

178. Seabrook, EYWTAASIW, pp. 171-175.

179. Seabrook, EYWTAASIW, pp. 48, 273, 549.

180. Seabrook, C101, passim. One must also ask why the South would want to "purposefully destroy the Union," as our fake history books teach, when it was the South herself who founded the Union to begin with? Thomas Jefferson wrote the Declaration of Independence, James Madison wrote the U.S. Constitution, and George Mason conceived the Bill of Rights (later written by Madison), the documents that form the very foundation of the U.S. All three men were from Virginia.

181. It is true, for example, that Sanders is a democratic socialist and Hitler was a national socialist. Yet their primary goal was and still is ultimately the same: a government-run society. Revealingly, Lenin went as far as to state that "the goal of socialism is communism." For more on this topic, see Seabrook, CFF, passim.

182. For more on this topic, see Seabrook, ALWALJDWAC, passim.

183. For more on this topic, see Seabrook, C101, passim.

184. Seabrook, VCP, p. 221.

185. *Confederate Veteran*, September 1905, Vol. 9, No. 6, p. 406.

186. See photo on page 290.

187. For more on Hazen's Monument, see *Confederate Veteran*, January 1897, Vol. 5, No. 1, p. 32.

188. One uninformed and bigoted Liberal, for example, Democrat Ruben Gallego of Arizona, has submitted a bill (H.R. 3007) to Congress "to prohibit the display of the Confederate Battle Flag in national cemeteries."

189. For more on Lincoln's racism, see Seabrook, AL, passim.

190. *Confederate Veteran*, January 1908, Vol. 16, No. 1, p. 49.

191. Seabrook, VCP, p. 384.

192. *Confederate Veteran*, October 1899, Vol. 7, No. 10, p. 457.

193. Emerson, p. 15.

194. French, pp. 402-403.

195. Emerson, p. 191.

196. *Confederate Veteran*, March 1917, Vol. 25, No. 3, cover.

197. *Confederate Veteran*, September 1916, Vol. 24, No. 9, cover.

198. Stiles, p. 20.

199. Emerson, pp. 294-295.

200. *Confederate Veteran*, June 1903, Vol. 11, No. 6, pp. 291-292.

201. *Confederate Veteran*, October 1908, Vol. 16, No. 10, p. 521.

202. Emerson, p. 26. Note: The title is mine.

203. Seabrook, RUACTB, pp. 492-497. My emphasis.

204. *Confederate Veteran*, June 1901, Vol. 9, No. 6, pp. 262-263. My emphasis.

205. Emerson, pp. 334, 336-337. My emphasis.

206. *Confederate Veteran*, August 1908, Vol. 16, No. 8, p. 377. My emphasis.

207. *Confederate Veteran*, August 1931, Vol. 39, No. 8, pp. 284-286.

208. *Confederate Veteran*, May 1898, Vol. 6, No. 5, p. 227.

209. *Confederate Veteran*, February 1928, Vol. 36, No. 2, p. 50. Note: President Coolidge also showed his respect for the Confederate soldier when gave a brief address (entitled "The United Nation") earlier, on May 25, 1924, at the Confederate Monument, Arlington National Cemetery, Arlington, Virginia.

210. *Confederate Veteran*, October 1922, Vol. 30, No. 11, p. 387.

211. Rutherford, Sec. 1, p. 4.

BIBLIOGRAPHY

Note: My pro-South readers are to be advised that the majority of the books listed here are anti-South in nature (some extremely so), and were written primarily by Liberal elitist, socialist, communist, and Marxist authors who loathe the South, and typically the United States and the U.S. Constitution as well. Despite this, as a scholar I find these titles indispensable, for *an honest evaluation of Lincoln's War is not possible without studying both the Southern and the Northern versions*—an attitude, unfortunately, completely lacking among pro-North historians (who read and study only their own ahistorical version). Still, it must be said that the material contained in these often mean-spirited works is largely the result of a century and a half of Yankee myth, falsehoods, cherry-picking, slander, redaction, sophistry, editorializing, anti-South propaganda, outright lies, and junk research, as modern pro-North writers merely copy one another's errors without ever looking at the original 19th-Century sources. This type of literature, filled as it is with both misinformation and disinformation, is called "scholarly" and "objective" by pro-North advocates. In the process, the mistakes and lies in these fact-free, fault-ridden, South-shaming, historically inaccurate works have been magnified over the years, and the North's version of the "Civil War" has come to be accepted as the only legitimate one. Indeed, it is now the only one known by most people. That over 95 percent of the titles in most of my bibliographies fall into the anti-South category is simply a reflection of the enormous power and influence that the pro-North movement—our nation's cultural ruling class—has long held over America's education system, libraries, publishing houses, and media (paper and electronic). My books serve as a small rampart against the overwhelming tide of anti-South Fascists, Liberals, cultural Marxists, and political elites, all who are working hard to obliterate Southern culture and guarantee that you will never learn the Truth about Lincoln and his War on the Constitution and the American people.

BENSON, AL, JR., and WALTER DONALD KENNEDY. *Lincoln's Marxists*. Gretna, LA: Pelican, 2011.

BOYD, JAMES P. *Parties, Problems, and Leaders of 1896: An Impartial Presentation of Living National Questions*. Chicago, IL: Publishers' Union, 1896.

BROCK, ROBERT ALONZO (ed.). *Southern Historical Society Papers*. 52 vols. Richmond, VA: Southern Historical Society, 1876-1943.

BROWDER, EARL. *Lincoln and the Communists*. New York, NY: Workers Library Publishers, Inc., 1936.

BRYAN, WILLIAM JENNINGS. *The First Battle: A Story of the Campaign of 1896*. Chicago, IL: W. B. Conkey Co., 1896.

BURNS, JAMES MACGREGOR. *The Vineyard of Liberty*. New York, NY: Alfred A. Knopf, 1982.

CHRISTIAN, GEORGE LLEWELLYN. *Abraham Lincoln: An Address Delivered Before R. E. Lee Camp, No. 1 Confederate Veterans at Richmond, VA, October 29, 1909*. Richmond, VA: L. H. Jenkins, 1909.

——. *A Capitol Disaster: A Chapter of Reconstruction in Virginia*. Richmond, VA: self-published, 1915.

——. *Confederate Memories and Experiences*. Richmond, VA: self-published, 1915.

Confederate Veteran (Sumner A. Cunningham, ed.). 40 vols. Nashville, TN: Confederate Veteran, 1893-1932.

DAVIS, JEFFERSON. *The Rise and Fall of the Confederate Government*. 2 vols. New

York, NY: D. Appleton and Co., 1881.

DAVIS, WILLIAM J. (ed.). *The Partisan Rangers of the Confederate States Army*. Louisville, KY: George G. Fetter Co., 1904.

EMERSON, BETTIE ALDER CALHOUN. *Historic Southern Monuments: Representative Memorials of the Heroic Dead of the Southern Confederacy*. New York, NY: Neale Publishing Co., 1911.

EVANS, CLEMENT ANSELM (ed.). *Confederate Military History*. 12 vols. Atlanta, GA: Confederate Publishing Co., 1899.

FRANKLIN, JOHN HOPE. *Reconstruction After the Civil War*. Chicago, IL: University of Chicago Press, 1961.

FRENCH, SAMUEL GIBBS. *Two Wars: An Autobiography of Gen. Samuel G. French*. Nashville, TN: Confederate Veteran, 1901.

GORDON, JOHN BROWN. *Reminiscences of the Civil War*. New York, NY: Charles Scribner's Sons, 1903.

JOHNSON, ROBERT UNDERWOOD, and CLARENCE CLOUGH BUEL (eds.). *Battles and Leaders of the Civil War*. 4 vols. New York, NY: The Century Co., 1884-1888.

JOHNSTONE, HUGER WILLIAM. *Truth of War Conspiracy, 1861*. Idylwild, GA: H. W. Johnstone, 1921.

JONES, JOHN WILLIAM. *The Davis Memorial Volume; Or Our Dead President, Jefferson Davis and the World's Tribute to His Memory*. Richmond, VA: B. F. Johnson, 1889.

KAPLAN, JUSTIN. *Mr. Clemens and Mark Twain: A Biography*. New York, NY: Simon and Schuster, 1966.

——. *Walt Whitman: A Life*. New York, NY: Simon and Schuster, 1980.

LIVERMORE, THOMAS L. *Numbers and Losses in the Civil War in America, 1861-65*. 1900. Carlisle, PA: John Kallmann, 1996 ed.

MAGLIOCCA, GERARD N. *The Tragedy of William Jennings Bryan: Constitutional Law and the Politics of Backlash*. New Haven, CT: Yale University Press, 2011.

MCCARTY, BURKE (ed.). *Little Sermons in Socialism by Abraham Lincoln*. Chicago, IL: The Chicago Daily Socialist, 1910.

MCLAUGHLIN, ANDREW C., and ALBERT BUSHNELL HART (eds.). *Cyclopedia of American Government*. 3 vols. New York, NY: D. Appleton and Co., 1914.

MCPHERSON, JAMES M. *Abraham Lincoln and the Second American Revolution*. New York, NY: Oxford University Press, 1991.

MERIWETHER, ELIZABETH AVERY (pseudonym, "George Edmonds"). *Facts and Falsehoods Concerning the War on the South, 1861-1865*. Memphis, TN: A. R. Taylor and Co., 1904.

MILLER, FRANCIS TREVELYAN, and ROBERT S. LANIER (eds.). *The Photographic History of the Civil War*. 10 vols. New York, NY: The Review of Reviews Co., 1911.

Minutes of the Eighth Annual Meeting and Reunion of the United Confederate Veterans, Atlanta, GA, July 20-23, 1898. New Orleans, LA: United Confederate Veterans, 1907.

Minutes of the Ninth Annual Meeting and Reunion of the United Confederate Veterans, Charleston, SC, May 10-13, 1899. New Orleans, LA: United Confederate Veterans, 1907.

Minutes of the Twelfth Annual Meeting and Reunion of the United Confederate Veterans, Dallas, TX, April 22-25, 1902. New Orleans, LA: United Confederate Veterans, 1907.

MISH, FREDERICK C. (ed.). *Webster's Ninth New Collegiate Dictionary*. 1828. Springfield, MA: Merriam-Webster, 1984 ed.

MUZZEY, DAVID SAVILLE. *The United States of America: Vol. 1, To the Civil War*. Boston, MA: Ginn and Co., 1922.

——. *The American Adventure: Vol. 2, From the Civil War*. 1924. New York, NY: Harper and Brothers, 1927 ed.

NICOLAY, JOHN G., and JOHN HAY (eds.). *Abraham Lincoln: A History*. 10 vols. New York, NY: The Century Co., 1890.

——. *Complete Works of Abraham Lincoln*. 12 vols. 1894. New York, NY: Francis D. Tandy Co., 1905 ed.

——. *Abraham Lincoln: Complete Works*. 12 vols. 1894. New York, NY: The Century Co., 1907 ed.

ORA (full title: *The War of the Rebellion: A Compilation of the Official Records of the Union and Confederate Armies*). 70 vols. Washington, DC: Government Printing Office, 1880.

ORN (full title: *Official Records of the Union and Confederate Navies in the War of the Rebellion*). 30 vols. Washington, DC: Government Printing Office, 1894.

POLLARD, EDWARD ALFRED. *The Lost Cause*. New York, NY: E. B. Treat and Co., 1867.

POLLEY, JOSEPH BENJAMIN. *A Soldier's Letters to Charming Nellie*. New York, NY: Neale Publishing Co., 1908.

RICHARDSON, JOHN ANDERSON. *Richardson's Defense of the South*. Atlanta, GA: A. B. Caldwell, 1914.

ROGERS, WILLIAM P. *The Three Secession Movements in the United States: Samuel J. Tilden, the Democratic Candidate for Presidency; the Advisor, Aider and Abettor of the Great Secession Movement of 1860; and One of the Authors of the Infamous Resolution of 1864; His Claims as a Statesman and Reformer Considered*. Boston, MA: John Wilson and Son, 1876.

ROVE, KARL. *The Triumph of William McKinley: Why the Election of 1896 Still Matters*. New York, NY: Simon and Schuster, 2015.

RUSSELL, PHILLIPS. *Emerson: The Wisest American*. New York, NY: Blue Ribbon Books, 1929.

RUTHERFORD, MILDRED LEWIS. *Truths of History: A Fair, Unbiased, Impartial, Unprejudiced and Conscientious Study of History*. Athens, GA: n.p., 1920.

SEABROOK, LOCHLAINN. *Carnton Plantation Ghost Stories: True Tales of the Unexplained from Tennessee's Most Haunted Civil War House!* 2005. Franklin, TN, 2016 ed.

——. *Nathan Bedford Forrest: Southern Hero, American Patriot*. 2007. Franklin, TN, 2010 ed.

——. *Abraham Lincoln: The Southern View*. 2007. Franklin, TN: Sea Raven Press, 2013 ed.

——. *The McGavocks of Carnton Plantation: A Southern History - Celebrating One of Dixie's Most Noble Confederate Families and Their Tennessee Home*. 2008. Franklin, TN, 2011ed.

——. *A Rebel Born: A Defense of Nathan Bedford Forrest*. 2010. Franklin, TN: Sea Raven Press, 2011 ed.

——. *A Rebel Born: The Screenplay* (for the film). 2011. Franklin, TN: Sea Raven Press.

——. *Everything You Were Taught About the Civil War is Wrong, Ask a Southerner!* 2010. Franklin, TN: Sea Raven Press, revised 2014 ed.

——. *The Quotable Jefferson Davis: Selections From the Writings and Speeches of the Confederacy's First President*. Franklin, TN: Sea Raven Press, 2011.

——. *The Quotable Robert E. Lee: Selections From the Writings and Speeches of the South's Most Beloved Civil War General*. Franklin, TN: Sea Raven Press, 2011 Sesquicentennial Civil War Edition.

——. *Lincolnology: The Real Abraham Lincoln Revealed In His Own Words*. Franklin, TN: Sea Raven Press, 2011.

——. *The Unquotable Abraham Lincoln: The President's Quotes They Don't Want You To Know!* Franklin, TN: Sea Raven Press, 2011.

——. *Honest Jeff and Dishonest Abe: A Southern Children's Guide to the Civil War*. Franklin, TN: Sea Raven Press, 2012.

——. *Encyclopedia of the Battle of Franklin - A Comprehensive Guide to the Conflict that Changed the Civil War*. Franklin, TN: Sea Raven Press, 2012.

——. *The Quotable Nathan Bedford Forrest: Selections From the Writings and Speeches of the Confederacy's Most Brilliant Cavalryman*. Spring Hill, TN: Sea Raven Press, 2012.

——. *Forrest! 99 Reasons to Love Nathan Bedford Forrest*. Spring Hill, TN: Sea Raven Press, 2012.

——. *Give 'Em Hell Boys! The Complete Military Correspondence of Nathan Bedford Forrest*. Spring Hill, TN: Sea Raven Press, 2012.

——. *The Constitution of the Confederate States of America Explained: A Clause-by-Clause Study of the South's Magna Carta*. Spring Hill, TN: Sea Raven Press, 2012 Sesquicentennial Civil War Edition.

——. *The Great Impersonator: 99 Reasons to Dislike Abraham Lincoln*. Spring Hill, TN: Sea Raven Press, 2012.

——. *The Old Rebel: Robert E. Lee As He Was Seen By His Contemporaries*. Spring Hill, TN: Sea Raven Press, 2012 Sesquicentennial Civil War Edition.

——. *The Quotable Stonewall Jackson: Selections From the Writings and Speeches of the South's Most Famous General*. Spring Hill, TN: Sea Raven Press, 2012 Sesquicentennial Civil War Edition.

——. *Saddle, Sword, and Gun: A Biography of Nathan Bedford Forrest for Teens*. Spring Hill, TN: Sea Raven Press, 2013.

——. *The Alexander H. Stephens Reader: Excerpts From the Works of a Confederate Founding Father*. Spring Hill, TN: Sea Raven Press, 2013.

———. *The Quotable Alexander H. Stephens: Selections From the Writings and Speeches of the Confederacy's First Vice President.* Spring Hill, TN: Sea Raven Press, 2013 Sesquicentennial Civil War Edition.

———. *Give This Book to a Yankee! A Southern Guide to the Civil War for Northerners.* Spring Hill, TN: Sea Raven Press, 2014.

———. *The Articles of Confederation Explained: A Clause-by-Clause Study of America's First Constitution.* Spring Hill, TN: Sea Raven Press, 2014.

———. *Confederate Blood and Treasure: An Interview With Lochlainn Seabrook.* Spring Hill, TN: Sea Raven Press, 2015.

———. *Nathan Bedford Forrest and the Battle of Fort Pillow: Yankee Myth, Confederate Fact.* Spring Hill, TN: Sea Raven Press, 2015.

———. *Everything You Were Taught About American Slavery War is Wrong, Ask a Southerner!* Spring Hill, TN: Sea Raven Press, 2015.

———. *Confederacy 101: Amazing Facts You Never Knew About America's Oldest Political Tradition.* Spring Hill, TN: Sea Raven Press, 2015.

———. *The Great Yankee Coverup: What the North Doesn't Want You to Know About Lincoln's War!* Spring Hill, TN: Sea Raven Press, 2015.

———. *Slavery 101: Amazing Facts You Never Knew About America's "Peculiar Institution."* Spring Hill, TN: Sea Raven Press, 2015.

———. *Confederate Flag Facts: What Every American Should Know About Dixie's Southern Cross.* Spring Hill, TN: Sea Raven Press, 2016.

———. *Nathan Bedford Forrest and the Ku Klux Klan: Yankee Myth, Confederate Fact.* Spring Hill, TN: Sea Raven Press, 2016.

———. *Seabrook's Bible Dictionary of Traditional and Mystical Christian Doctrines.* Spring Hill, TN: Sea Raven Press, 2016.

———. *Everything You Were Taught About African-Americans and the Civil War is Wrong, Ask a Southerner!* Spring Hill, TN: Sea Raven Press, 2016.

———. *Nathan Bedford Forrest and African-Americans: Yankee Myth, Confederate Fact.* Spring Hill, TN: Sea Raven Press, 2016.

———. *Women in Gray: A Tribute to the Ladies Who Supported the Southern Confederacy.* Spring Hill, TN: Sea Raven Press, 2016.

———. *Lincoln's War: The Real Cause, the Real Winner, the Real Loser.* Spring Hill, TN: Sea Raven Press, 2016.

———. *The Unholy Crusade: Lincoln's Legacy of Destruction in the American South.* Spring Hill, TN: Sea Raven Press, 2017.

———. *Abraham Lincoln Was a Liberal, Jefferson Davis Was a Conservative: The Missing Key to Understanding the American Civil War.* Spring Hill, TN: Sea Raven Press, 2017.

———. *All We Ask is to be Let Alone: The Southern Secession Fact Book.* Spring Hill, TN: Sea Raven Press, 2017.

———. *The Ultimate Civil War Quiz Book: How Much Do You Really Know About America's Most Misunderstood Conflict?* Spring Hill, TN: Sea Raven Press, 2017.

———. *Rise Up and Call Them Blessed: Victorian Tributes to the Confederate Soldier, 1861-1901.* Spring Hill, TN: Sea Raven Press, 2017.

——. *Victorian Confederate Poetry: The Southern Cause in Verse, 1861-1901*. Spring Hill, TN: Sea Raven Press, 2018.

STEEL, SAMUEL AUGUSTUS. *The South Was Right*. Columbia, SC: R. L. Bryan Co., 1914.

STEPHENS, ALEXANDER HAMILTON. *Speech of Mr. Stephens, of Georgia, on the War and Taxation*. Washington, D.C.: J & G. Gideon, 1848.

——. *A Constitutional View of the Late War Between the States; Its Causes, Character, Conduct and Results*. 2 vols. Philadelphia, PA: National Publishing, Co., 1870.

——. *Recollections of Alexander H. Stephens: His Diary Kept When a Prisoner at Fort Warren, Boston Harbour, 1865*. New York, NY: Doubleday, Page, and Co., 1910.

STILES, ROBERT. *Four Years Under Marse Robert*. New York, NY: Neale Publishing Co., 1904.

THOMPSON, HOLLAND. *The New South: A Chronicle of Social and Industrial Evolution*. New Haven, CT: Yale University Press, 1920.

WARNER, EZRA J. *Generals in Gray: Lives of the Confederate Commanders*. 1959. Baton Rouge, LA: Louisiana State University Press, 1989 ed.

——. *Generals in Blue: Lives of the Union Commanders*. 1964. Baton Rouge, LA: Louisiana State University Press, 2006 ed.

WOODS, THOMAS E., JR. *The Politically Incorrect Guide to American History*. Washington, D.C.: Regnery, 2004.

INDEX

MEET THE AUTHOR

OCHLAINN SEABROOK, a neo-Victorian and world acclaimed man of letters, is a Kentucky Colonel and the winner of the prestigious Jefferson Davis Historical Gold Medal for his "masterpiece," *A Rebel Born: A Defense of Nathan Bedford Forrest*. A classic littérateur and an unreconstructed Southern historian, he is an award-winning author, Civil War scholar, Confederate culture expert, Bible authority, the leading popularizer of American Civil War history, and a traditional Southern Agrarian of Scottish, English, Irish, Dutch, Welsh, German, and Italian extraction.

A child prodigy, Seabrook is today a true Renaissance Man whose occupational titles also include encyclopedist, lexicographer, musician, artist, graphic designer, genealogist, photographer, and award-winning poet. Also a songwriter and a screenwriter, he has a 40 year background in historical nonfiction writing and is a member of the Sons of Confederate Veterans, the Civil War Trust, and the National Grange.

COPYRIGHT ©
SEA RAVEN PRESS

Above, Colonel Lochlainn Seabrook, "the voice of the traditional South," award-winning Civil War scholar and unreconstructed Southern historian. America's most popular and prolific pro-South author, his many books have introduced hundreds of thousands to the truth about the War for Southern Independence. He coined the phrase "South-shaming" and holds the world record for writing the most books on Nathan Bedford Forrest: ten.

Known to his many fans as the "voice of the traditional South," due to similarities in their writing styles, ideas, and literary works, Seabrook is also often referred to as the "new Shelby Foote," the "Southern Joseph Campbell," and the "American Robert Graves" (his English cousin). Seabrook coined the terms "South-shaming" and "Lincolnian liberalism," and holds the world's record for writing the most books on Nathan Bedford Forrest: ten. In addition, Seabrook is the first Civil War scholar to connect the early American nickname for the U.S., "The Confederate States of America," with the Southern Confederacy that arose eight decades later, and the first to note that in 1860 the party platforms of the two major political parties were the opposite of what they are today (Victorian Democrats were Conservatives, Victorian Republicans were Liberals).

The grandson of an Appalachian coal-mining family, Seabrook is a seventh-generation Kentuckian whose European ancestors came from Virginia, North Carolina, and Tennessee, settling in the Bluegrass State in the early 1700s, thereafter spreading into West Virginia, the Midwest, and finally the West.

Seabrook is co-chair of the Jent/Gent Family Committee (Kentucky), founder and director of the Blakeney Family Tree Project, and a board member of the Friends of Colonel Benjamin E. Caudill. His literary works have been endorsed by leading authorities, museum curators, award-winning historians, bestselling authors, celebrities, noted scientists, well regarded educators, TV show hosts and producers, renowned military artists, esteemed Southern organizations, and distinguished academicians from around the world.

Seabrook has authored over 50 popular adult books on the American Civil War, American and international slavery, the U.S. Confederacy (1781), the Southern Confederacy (1861), religion, theology, thealogy, Jesus, the Bible, the Apocrypha, the Law of Attraction, alternative health, spirituality, ghost stories, the paranormal, ufology, social issues, and cross-cultural studies of the family and marriage. His Confederate biographies, pro-South studies, genealogical monographs, family histories, military encyclopedias, self-help guides, and etymological dictionaries have received wide acclaim.

Seabrook's eight children's books include a Southern guide to the Civil War, a biography of Nathan Bedford Forrest, a dictionary of religion and myth, a rewriting of the King Arthur legend (which reinstates the original pre-Christian motifs), two bedtime stories for preschoolers, a naturalist's guidebook to owls, a worldwide look at the family, and an examination of the Near-Death Experience.

Of blue-blooded Southern stock through his Kentucky, Tennessee, Virginia, North Carolina and West Virginia ancestors, he is a direct descendant of European royalty via his 6th great-grandfather, the Earl of Oxford, after which London's famous Harley Street is named. Among his celebrated male Celtic ancestors is Robert the Bruce, King of Scotland, Seabrook's 22nd great-grandfather. The 21st great-grandson of Edward I "Longshanks" Plantagenet), King of England, Seabrook is a 17th-generation Southerner through his descent from the colonists of Jamestown, Virginia (1607).

(Photo © Lochlainn Seabrook)

The 2nd, 3rd, and 4th great-grandson of dozens of Confederate soldiers, one of his closest connections to Lincoln's War is through his 3rd great-grandfather, Elias Jent, Sr., who fought for the Confederacy in the Thirteenth Cavalry Kentucky under Seabrook's 2nd cousin, Colonel Benjamin E. Caudill. The Thirteenth, also known as "Caudill's Army," fought in numerous conflicts, including the Battles of Saltville, Gladsville, Mill Cliff, Poor Fork, Whitesburg, and Leatherwood.

Seabrook is a direct descendant of the families of Alexander H. Stephens, John Singleton Mosby, William Giles Harding, and Edmund Winchester Rucker, and is related to the following Confederates and other 18th- and 19th-Century luminaries: Robert E. Lee, Stephen Dill Lee, Stonewall Jackson, Nathan Bedford Forrest, James Longstreet, John Hunt Morgan, Jeb Stuart, Pierre G. T. Beauregard (approved the Confederate Battle Flag design), George W. Gordon, John Bell Hood, Alexander Peter Stewart, Arthur M. Manigault, Joseph Manigault, Charles Scott Venable, Thornton A. Washington, John A. Washington, Abraham Buford, Edmund W. Pettus, Theodrick "Tod" Carter, John B. Womack, John H. Winder, Gideon J. Pillow, States Rights Gist, Henry R. Jackson, John Lawton Seabrook, John C. Breckinridge, Leonidas Polk, Zachary Taylor, Sarah Knox Taylor (first wife of Jefferson Davis), Richard Taylor, Davy Crockett, Daniel Boone, Meriwether Lewis (of the Lewis and Clark Expedition) Andrew Jackson,

James K. Polk, Abram Poindexter Maury (founder of Franklin, TN), Zebulon Baird Vance, Thomas Jefferson, Edmund Jennings Randolph, George Wythe Randolph (grandson of Jefferson), Felix K. Zollicoffer, Fitzhugh Lee, Nathaniel F. Cheairs, Jesse James, Frank James, Robert Brank Vance, Charles Sidney Winder, John W. McGavock, Caroline E. (Winder) McGavock, David Harding McGavock, Lysander McGavock, James Randal McGavock, Randal William McGavock, Francis McGavock, Emily McGavock, William Henry F. Lee, Lucius E. Polk, Minor Meriwether (husband of noted pro-South author Elizabeth Avery Meriwether), Ellen Bourne Tynes (wife of Forrest's chief of artillery, Captain John W. Morton), South Carolina Senators Preston Smith Brooks and Andrew Pickens Butler, and famed South Carolina diarist Mary Chesnut.

Seabrook's modern day cousins include: Patrick J. Buchanan (conservative author), Cindy Crawford (model), Shelby Lee Adams (Letcher Co., Kentucky, photographer), Bertram Thomas Combs (Kentucky's 50th governor), Edith Bolling (second wife of President Woodrow Wilson), and actors Andy Griffith, Riley Keough, George C. Scott, Robert Duvall, Reese Witherspoon, Lee Marvin, Rebecca Gayheart, and Tom Cruise.

Seabrook's screenplay, *A Rebel Born*, based on his book of the same name, has been signed with acclaimed filmmaker Christopher Forbes (of Forbes Film). It is now in pre-production, and is set for release in 2018 as a full-length feature film. This will be the

first movie ever made of Nathan Bedford Forrest's life story, and as a historically accurate project written from the Southern perspective, is destined to be one of the most talked about Civil War films of all time.

Born with music in his blood, Seabrook is an award-winning, multi-genre, BMI-Nashville songwriter and lyricist who has composed some 3,000 songs (250 albums), and whose original music has been heard in film (*A Rebel Born, Cowgirls 'n Angels, Confederate Cavalry, Billy the Kid: Showdown in Lincoln County, Vengeance Without Mercy, Last Step, County Line, The Mark*) and on TV and radio worldwide. A musician, producer, multi-instrumentalist, and renown performer—whose keyboard work has been variously compared to pianists from Hargus Robbins and Vince Guaraldi to Elton John and Leonard Bernstein—Seabrook has opened for groups such as the Earl Scruggs Review, Ted Nugent, and Bob Seger, and has performed privately for such public figures as President Ronald Reagan, Burt Reynolds, Loni Anderson, and Senator Edward W. Brooke. Seabrook's cousins in the music business include: Johnny Cash, Elvis Presley, Lisa Marie Presley, Billy Ray and Miley Cyrus, Patty Loveless, Tim McGraw, Lee Ann Womack, Dolly Parton, Pat Boone, Naomi, Wynonna, and Ashley Judd, Ricky Skaggs, the Sunshine Sisters, Martha Carson, and Chet Atkins.

Seabrook lives with his wife and family in historic Middle Tennessee, the heart of Forrest country and the Confederacy, where his conservative Southern ancestors fought valiantly against Liberal Lincoln and the progressive North in defense of Jeffersonianism, constitutional government, and personal liberty.

LochlainnSeabrook.com

If you enjoyed this book you will be interested in Colonel Seabrook's other popular related titles:

- ☛ EVERYTHING YOU WERE TAUGHT ABOUT THE CIVIL WAR IS WRONG, ASK A SOUTHERNER!
- ☛ ABRAHAM LINCOLN WAS A LIBERAL, JEFFERSON DAVIS WAS A CONSERVATIVE
- ☛ ALL WE ASK IS TO BE LET ALONE: THE SOUTHERN SECESSION FACT BOOK
- ☛ EVERYTHING YOU WERE TAUGHT ABOUT AMERICAN SLAVERY IS WRONG, ASK A SOUTHERNER!
- ☛ CONFEDERATE FLAG FACTS: WHAT EVERY AMERICAN SHOULD KNOW ABOUT DIXIE'S SOUTHERN CROSS
- ☛ LINCOLN'S WAR: THE REAL CAUSE, THE REAL WINNER, THE REAL LOSER

Available from Sea Raven Press and wherever fine books are sold

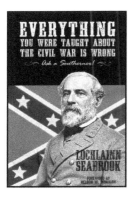

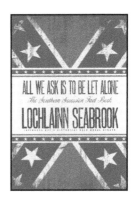

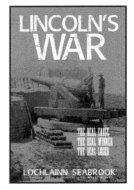

ALL OF OUR BOOK COVERS ARE AVAILABLE AS 11" X 17" POSTERS, SUITABLE FOR FRAMING

SeaRavenPress.com • NathanBedfordForrestBooks.com

Lightning Source UK Ltd.
Milton Keynes UK
UKHW041829250822
407860UK00002B/98